Saints
as
Citizens

Saints
as
Citizens

*A Guide
to Public Responsibilities
for Christians*

**Timothy R. Sherratt
& Ronald P. Mahurin**

Foreword by James W. Skillen

The Center for Public Justice
Washington, DC 20002

BakerBooks
A Division of Baker Book House Co
Grand Rapids, Michigan 49516

© 1995 by Timothy R. Sherratt and Ronald P. Mahurin

Published by Baker Books
a division of Baker Book House Company
P.O. Box 6287, Grand Rapids, MI 49516–6287

Printed in the United States of America

Library of Congress Cataloging-in-Publication Data

Sherratt, Timothy R.
    Saints as citizens : a guide to public responsibilities for Christians / Timothy R. Sherratt and Ronald P. Mahurin.
      p.   cm.
    Includes bibliographical references.
    ISBN 0-8010-8389-3
    1. Christianity and politics—Protestant churches. 2. Evangelicalism—United States—History—20th century. 3. United States—Politics and government—1945-1989. I. Mahurin, Ronald P. II. Title.
BR115.P7S464 1995
261.7—dc20   94-23996

For Christine and Jerilyn, authentic saints

Contents

Foreword by James W. Skillen   9
Acknowledgments   13

1 Sojourners and Citizens   15
2 Taking Our Bearings from the Kingdom   27
3 Setting Sail in the Church   43
4 Beyond Piecemeal Politics   57
5 Overcoming the Language Barrier   75
6 Christian Principles for Politics   95

Notes   121

Foreword

There is a close connection between the quality of life inside the household of faith and the degree of obedience to God demonstrated by believers in all areas of their life. How can we not be stunned by the prophet Isaiah's words from God to Israel:

> I cannot bear your evil assemblies.
> Your New Moon festivals and your appointed feasts
>   my soul hates.
> They have become a burden to me;
>   I am weary of bearing them.
> When you spread out your hands in prayer,
>   I will hide my eyes from you;
> even if you offer many prayers,
>   I will not listen.
> Your hands are full of blood;
>   wash and make yourselves clean.
> Take your evil deeds
>   out of my sight!
> Stop doing wrong,
>   learn to do right!
> Seek justice,
>   encourage the oppressed.

> Defend the cause of the fatherless,
> plead the case of the widow.
>   Isaiah 1:13–17 NIV

Was God telling Israel to quit praying and to give up Sabbath rest and worship? Of course not. Rather, God was telling the people of Israel that they could not carry on a relationship with him through worship services while they dishonored God's commandments on the other six days of the week. Doing justice is as urgent as offering prayers and sacrifices. The two go together because the same God has commanded both of them.

Tim Sherratt and Ron Mahurin render an important service to Christians in this book by showing why the life of any congregation of believers must be oriented to a full life of obedience to God. "God talk" cannot be restricted to private enclaves. Service to God in Christ entails more than worship and evangelism. The very authenticity of the church demands that it be about repentance from evil deeds, service to the needy and oppressed, and the search for justice.

From the point of view of life in the political arena there are thousands of important issues that Christians should be considering together very carefully in order to learn how best to do justice and to serve their neighbors. But this can be done properly only if Christians know who they are as a community of Christ's disciples. It is as Christ's followers, as members of the body of Christ, that believers bear a uniquely Christian responsibility in public life. To learn what that means, believers must know what life in Christ is all about.

This is the burden of the New Testament letter to the Hebrews. The author of that letter is concerned about the immaturity of Christ's followers, who run the danger of falling away from faithful obedience because they are still infants needing milk when they should be mature enough to eat solid food. What does it mean to be a mature Christian? According to Hebrews, mature believers are those who by constant practice "have trained themselves to distinguish good from evil" (5:14 NIV).

Later on in the letter, the author urges believers to "consider how we may spur one another on toward love and good deeds. Let us not give up meeting together, as some are in the habit of doing, but let us encourage one another—and all the more as you see the Day approaching" (10:24–25 NIV). What should bring Christians together? Only occasions for worship and prayer? No, Christians should also be gathering together—locking arms in encouragement and mutual support—to spur one another on toward love and good deeds. By constant practice, including organized means, Christians must train themselves to distinguish good from evil in all areas of life, including the political arena where they bear civic responsibility. This should be as natural for Christians as eating and drinking to the glory of God. Doing justice does not involve some tricky or hard-to-justify departure from the proper and ordinary life of the church. The authors are convinced that the pursuit of public justice is an integral part of the church's true life and identity, an integral part of living the Christian life to the full.

Christian community begins in repentance at the foot of the cross, in awe-filled prayer before the empty tomb, in exuberant celebration on the Day of Pentecost. The community of Christ's disciples comes to maturity as its members train through prayer, worship, and sustained activity to spur one another on toward love and good deeds—in public life as well as in personal relationships, in doing justice as well as in practicing charity.

Saints as Citizens is just the book for Christians who feel comfortable gathering for worship on Sunday but who may feel uncertain about how they should act in public as Christ's disciples. If you believe in prayer, praise, and evangelism but feel uncomfortable about, or even disgusted with, the way some Christians conduct themselves in the political arena, then read the pages that follow. And as you keep on gathering with other believers for worship, do so as a disciple who acknowledges that God has called you to grow to maturity in Christ, to pursue justice, to learn to distinguish good from evil as a citizen. All of this, and not only worship, requires a cooperative effort of spurring one another on to love and good deeds in both public and private life, in both politics and evangelism.

James W. Skillen
Executive Director
Center for Public Justice

Acknowledgments

Many people helped bring *Saints as Citizens* to fruition. Thank you to parishioners at All Saints' Episcopal Church, West Newbury, Massachusetts, for insights and ideas in the Sunday school class that launched the project; to the many students at Gordon College who responded to the book's themes as we explored them in "Power and Justice: Perspectives on Political Order"; to Steve Comley, who was gracious in sharing his own courageous journey into the politics of the nuclear industry; to the Movement for Christian Democracy in Great Britain for affording Tim Sherratt the opportunity to sit in on their deliberations in 1992—thanks especially to Robert Song, Christopher Graffius, David Alton, MP, and Alan Storkey; to colleagues and friends at Gordon; to Harry Durning for his sustained interest in what we were doing; and to the college administration for its sabbatical leave policy, which helped us finish the manuscript. We owe our heaviest debt to Jim Skillen for his editorial advice and above all for his unfailing encouragement. We are delighted that the book is being published jointly by Baker Book House

13

and the Center for Public Justice, which he directs. All of these people have helped; responsibility for opinions expressed here is ours alone.

Finally, we want to thank our editors, Dan Van't Kerkhoff and Mary Suggs, and all the staff at Baker Book House for their hard work, patience, and cooperation in producing the book.

1

Sojourners and Citizens

How are Christians to navigate the often stormy waters of public life? That's a question long overdue now that we have some perspective on the "Christian politics" of the last twenty years. For after decades of remaining firmly at anchor in the safe havens of their churches, evangelical Christians finally set sail in the 1970s.

The answer as to how Christians have navigated through public life is not an encouraging one. After two decades of public activity, many evangelicals can point proudly to their public efforts: backing presidential candidates, organizing voter registration drives, penetrating state party organizations, campaigning for prayer in the public schools, or taking up the struggle against abortion on demand. It is abundantly clear, however, that these same evangelicals used no sophisticated navigational equipment at all to find their way politically; they still do their politics piecemeal, on an issue-by-issue basis, and this is discouraging for several reasons.

First, piecemeal politics is likely to be reactive rather than creative. Government acts, Christians react. Political parties, special interest groups, or the events themselves set the agenda, make the rules, and dictate the "realities" involved, leaving Christians scrambling to frame an adequate response. We could call this political crisis management. But should Christian politics be crisis management? Shouldn't Christians base their politics on Christian principles?

Second, because it is too reactive and spasmodic to have developed a set of Christian principles, piecemeal politics "borrows" principles from outside the faith. This borrowing is not inevitably bad, but when it is indiscriminate its consequences can severely compromise Christian witness. Take party politics, for example. In its present state, it offers choices that make for a clumsy fit with Christian faith. "Republican" or "Democratic," "liberal" or "conservative"—none of these terms is a satisfactory substitute for "Christian," yet without a Christian framework to draw on, the temptation to make do with one or more of these usually proves too strong to resist. The borrowed framework may turn into a straitjacket if taken to extremes.

Third, piecemeal politics means that for all their activity and experience, evangelicals may never develop a permanent commitment to governing; at best they will try to subject society to occasional reforms. But the Bible contains many examples of administrators as reformers. And the reformers, particularly the prophets, actually call God's people to just administration, urging them to pursue justice. Even when they call for major course corrections, the prophets affirm the need for a steady hand on the tiller at all times.

The piecemeal politics of the 1980s should have come as no surprise to one familiar with the history of evangelical churches in the United States. Two distinctly American characteristics, one religious and the other political, have contributed to the style and substance of contemporary evangelical political action. The religious characteristic is the denomination, whose widespread appearance and the tolerance it engendered can fairly be called America's distinctive contribution to the church's history. Nurtured in the soil of American religious pluralism, denominations represent both a unique flowering of religious liberty—for they have blossomed in numbers and varieties unheard of elsewhere—and a drastic pruning of the New Testament idea of the church. Retreating from the many-faceted image of Christ's body in the world, denominations have contented themselves with the status of private associations of like-minded believers.

The distinctive political characteristic shaping evangelical politics is the separation of church and state—which, in its American form, has guaranteed nearly absolute religious freedom for individuals but has confined religious expression largely to their private lives. In combination, these two characteristics, of which we will have more to say later, have made it enormously difficult for American Christians to build an edifice of political responsibility any more sophisticated than the temporary shacks from which piecemeal politics is dispensed. Privatized churches and official discouragement of "sectarian" activity in the public square are uninviting conditions in which to develop an attitude, much less a philosophy, of ongoing Christian responsibility in politics.

To pursue our nautical metaphor, evangelicals did not set sail in the 1980s without clearly defined purposes. Indeed, they invoked a venerable tradition of evangelical social criticism and reform stretching back a century or more on both sides of the Atlantic.[1] But they generally operated without the sophisticated navigational equipment that befits a determination to press on at all seasons and in all weather. The vessels they crewed were built for the quiet backwaters of private life and, despite innovative retrofitting, proved quite unfit for the high seas of state and national politics.

We think that an authentic, fully orbed Christianity must take its bearings with great care, must employ navigational equipment that is up to the task, and must voyage in the right sort of vessel. Only then will evangelicals get past an issue-by-issue approach to public life. Only then will they stop viewing the public arena as an unnatural place for a Christian. Only then will they be able to place the calling to permanent service alongside existing traditions of periodic reform.

Sojourner

At first sight, the call to "permanent public service" may seem controversial from a biblical point of view, quite apart from evangelical traditions. Consider Paul's words to the Ephesians: "You are no longer strangers and sojourners, but you are fellow citizens with the saints and members of the household of God" (Eph. 2:19). A sojourner is a resident alien, one who lives among a people with whom he or she shares much but who seeks full citizenship in another society. He is Abraham, living with his sons in tents but looking forward to "the city which has foundations, whose builder and maker is God" (Heb. 11:10). The great "cloud of witnesses" in the letter to the Hebrews "desire a better country, that is, a heavenly one" (11:16). That country or city (the words being used quite interchangeably) is the heavenly city. In Christian tradition, entry into the heavenly city is to be most highly valued; alongside it, membership in another society is a poor substitute.

Many statements in the New Testament—a good number of them made by Jesus—remind believers that they are not of the world, despite their sojourn in it. Jesus' teaching in John 16 and his prayer in the following chapter exemplify these Scriptures. Paul's well-known exhortation to the church at Rome—"Do not be conformed to this world but be transformed by the renewal of your mind" (Rom. 12:2)—strikes a similar note, as do John's warnings to test the spirits to discern which are worldly (1 John 4:1–6). These particular passages identify the world rather strongly with evil; others speak to a prudent detachment from worldly affairs simply on account of the imminent return of Christ. Paul even urges, "let those who have wives live as though they had none" (1 Cor. 7:29), for example. So, then, does the very status of sojourner undercut our case for Christian responsibilities in public affairs at the outset?

The sojourner possesses the perspective of one whose stay is temporary, who lives in the middle of a culture but cannot make its mores his own, who may come to know with every passing year that familiarity with a society is not the same as full membership and is never likely to make a satisfactory substitute for it. At the same time, however, familiarity may develop in the sojourner great affection, penetrating criticism, and insights free from cultural taboos. If the Christian stands in this sojourning relationship to the world, as the writer of Hebrews suggests, his or her responsibility to the world can never be an empty one. There can be no thought of simply passing through without giving something back. The lessons the world has to teach are not for personal edification alone. The sojourner, an honored guest in those Middle Eastern societies that do not grant him citizenship, has something to offer the host society precisely by virtue of his status on its periphery.

Citizen

If sojourning were the only way to see a Christian's relationship to the world, our book might be at most a plea for its readers to take some interest in the world, to learn about politics, to make their learning available to the church, and to not leave political education entirely to secular "experts." Yet each of us is also a citizen. We live in real towns, counties, states, provinces, and nations. Perhaps it is exactly because of our sojourner status that the Scriptures take great pains to discuss our responsibilities to these temporal domains. Governing authorities receive great respect from Paul because government is ordained by God (Rom. 13). Jesus himself taught that the offices of government have rightful demands to make of us (Luke 20:20–26). Strong traditions, both Catholic and Protestant, affirm Christian calling to the administration of civil society. Everyone has some civic responsibilities; for some, these amount to a lifework, a vocation.

Moreover, although we might be inclined to equate the term *citizen* with conceptions of society foreign to Christian community—it is certainly an older term than the Christian *oikoumenē*—we ought to recall that the Bible depicts human communities as developing from the bucolic Garden of Eden to the heavenly city at the end of the age. In the context of the "creation mandate" (as Reformed tradition refers to it) to cultivate, or care for, the earth, the office of citizen confers distinct obligations. The mark of a citizen, Aristotle taught, was that he (Aristotle restricted citizenship to men) *participates* in the administration of society, holding office in rotation with fellow citizens. No halfhearted minimal participation this; mere voting in the infrequent elections of our own democracy would not have qualified a person for the title of citizen. Citizens hold office.

If Christ's redemption is to be taken seriously as a "buying back" of fallen humanity, we must consider that we fell from our God-given office of caring for the created order. We became its irresponsible exploiters instead. To return to responsibility, we must take our participatory obligations seriously. They are set by the creation story itself!

If Christians are not just temporary residents but sojourner-citizens, and if the prospect of substantial responsibility and love for our fellow humans arises from both parts of this status, then we will want to take our bearings from it accurately and often. In chapter 2 we will try to show that Jesus' teachings on the kingdom are of fundamental importance to giving our public responsibilities their distinctively Christian shape, and in chapter 3 we will urge Christians to grapple with the theology and sociology of the church for the same reasons.

Jesus' teachings on the kingdom are his principal teachings. As such, they unfold the gospel hope on a scale and in a form that lays the foundation for a Christian public philosophy. These teachings proclaim the good news of the reality of God's sovereignty over the whole face of life. They embrace but extend beyond

the promise of personal salvation and the call to personal morality. Christians must take seriously the as-
tonishing claims of Jesus that the kingdom, sown in
the world, embraces the new reality of God's sovereignty, a new loyalty to the implications of that sovereignty, and a new ethic of just distribution and re-
ciprocal forgiveness. This is the Good News! But only
by living in its light will we position ourselves to defend a faith on the scale of our inheritance in Christ.
To proclaim the gospel hope and defend the faith
(1 Peter 3:15) on any lesser scale is to fall short of Peter's
urging that Christians always be prepared to make a
defense of our hope in Christ.

As for the church, our discussion will be both theological and political/sociological. The image of the
church we have in mind is the body of Christ, a view
that conveys both a personal relationship with Jesus
and the mystical continuity and connectedness of
Christ's followers down through the ages. The body of
Christ takes us out into the world in a way that neither
the sect form of radical Protestantism nor the denominational form of evangelical Protestantism can. Either
of these forms may suffer undue privatization. America has been home to both. As a result, American
churches have tended not to resemble the true church—
that is, the body of Christ—at all. Instead, they have
willingly accepted a drab utilitarian status of private
groups of believers.

Only so much can be done to correct this ambiva-
lence to public responsibility. This is to be a practical
guidebook, so we won't harp on the "if onlys." But if
we are to set sail in the church, we must know the
church's limitations, and we must learn how to encourage our own congregations to recover in practical
fashion the authentic biblical way of life.

Conclusion

The primary motivation behind this book is to try to supply a guide to Christians' public responsibilities, not to oversimplify a complex reality. We have no simple formula for politics in four laws or five principles or twelve steps, notwithstanding the value of such formulas in their proper seasons and places. Nor are we interested in destructive criticism of the efforts of fellow Christians. Their struggles, successes, and failures furnish many a useful moral for our tale, however, and we shall not hesitate to acknowledge them in this spirit.

A word about sailing. Neither of us is a sailor—we are both trained as political scientists—but we persist in using sailing expressions all the same. Why? Well, you cannot be a Christian for any length of time, and you cannot read and study politics for any length of time, without being drawn to the nautical metaphors that pervade both. From Aristotle's famous "ship of state" in fragile dependence on its steering oar, to James's caustic observations about the tongue as the rudder of the human soul, to the disciples themselves "making headway painfully" against the Galilean wind and their own opacity to the teachings of Jesus, to the old and affectionate nickname for the Catholic Church (the Barque of Saint Peter), political philosophers and Christians have turned to ships and the sea to make their meanings clear. We will invoke this venerable tradition, confident in its power to illustrate and clarify.

Sailors we are not, but Protestants, and evangelical ones at that, we are indeed. As such we are also, like every other Protestant who has ever lived, partial and susceptible to the neat formula, the tidy argument, the fundamentals of the faith laid out clearly. Reformed

theology and philosophy, to which we owe no small
debt for marshaling our thoughts into the chapters of
this book, can also creep into our arguments. So just in
case you, or we, seem to get carried away by our
metaphors into an artificial clarity and precision that
misrepresents the teachings of Jesus, we recall the remark attributed to President Taft when a young aide
waxed lyrical about the "machinery" of government:
"You know," Taft is reputed to have whispered to a
nearby friend, "he really thinks it *is* a machine." Taft's
remark is well taken. No one who has tried to grapple
seriously with Jesus' teachings is entitled to be so glib
with them—especially the parables, which comprise the
bulk and the heart of his teachings—as to pass them off
as pithy sayings with accompanying illustrations. No
more may we. Even though we offer this work as a
guide, we dissent from the how-to format and would
prefer that our readers look for basic direction to our
central themes, necessary and foundational perhaps,
but hardly a black box of Christian answers to tough
political questions, and certainly not sufficient in themselves to render further group and personal study on
the subject superfluous. Quite to the contrary, we have
written this book for church study groups in particular,
as well as college students, whose questions echo
through these pages and compel us to rethink our answers again and again.

STUDY QUESTIONS

   1. What is "Christian politics"? Can there be such a
      thing? For example, what do you make of efforts
      by Christians to take over state party organiza-

tions, as they have done in Virginia's Republican Party in the early 1990s?

2. How does the biblical status of "sojourner" for the believer shed light on what Christian public responsibility might entail?

3. What are the obligations of citizens in American society? Should these obligations be more or less extensive?

4. Do you agree with the authors that sojourners make good citizens?

2

Taking Our Bearings from the Kingdom

In this chapter we will discuss the importance of Jesus' teachings on the kingdom for Christian public responsibility. Our discussion's focal points will include the Lord's Prayer, the miracles recorded in Matthew's Gospel, and the parables of the kingdom, for in all of these a theology of the kingdom unfolds. We believe this theology, this biblical account, has direct, immediate, and lasting implications for communities of Christians at the end of the twentieth century.

The teachings on the kingdom are beacons from which Christians ought to take their bearings. They give vital direction to the public enterprise, for from them we learn of God's relationship to the world, once created, now fallen. These teachings introduce us to God's power and to the way he chooses to exercise it, and they provide us an initiation into the norms of Christian justice.

Those looking for an exhaustive treatment on the theology of the kingdom will need to consult other works. The discussion that follows is meant to provide what philosophers call first principles, a scriptural foundation on which we shall develop our analysis, illustrations, and suggestions.

The Kingdom Motif in North American Churches

To provide a context for our discussion, consider how the kingdom motif has been employed in evangelical preaching and teaching in North America. Three ideas are common in the large number of works evangelical Christians have written on the subject of the kingdom. The first grasps the kingdom in solely future-oriented terms, the second in strictly spiritual terms, and the third in metaphorical terms so ambiguous that their value as a guide to Christian thought and life is called into question. Let's consider each of these ideas briefly.

The Strictly Future Kingdom

It comes as no surprise that in North American evangelical churches, preaching, teaching, and discussion on the kingdom of God tend to be oriented around eschatological concerns. After all, when Jesus says, "My kingship is not from the world" (John 18:36), Christians on the fringes of society (or being pushed to its fringes) have eagerly understood him to mean that the kingdom must be otherworldly in either space ("spiritual" rather than "earthly") or time (a kingdom still to come). Corroborated as it is by Jesus' instruction that the disciples should pray for the coming of the kingdom, the idea of a strictly future kingdom has taken its place in evangelical understanding. This future orientation links the kingdom with the return of Christ.

More loosely, this future kingdom is associated with heaven, a view strengthened by Matthew's usage of the term "kingdom of heaven" throughout the Gospel that bears his name. When one turns to Jesus' teachings on the kingdom of heaven, illustration after illustration is drawn from nature and daily life—the sower, the mustard seed, the lost coin, and so forth. Even so, in the hands of many evangelical interpreters, the kingdom of heaven manifests little connection with or concern for this fallen world. The stricter the future orientation, the more likely the evangelical or fundamentalist interpreters will speak of the devastating judgment of God upon the fallen nations of the world. The horrors of the nuclear age furnish an appropriately apocalyptic end for the world. In this context, the question begged is this: If the kingdom is a heavenly kingdom, why on earth should we worry about it?

The strictly future orientation is found in those evangelical churches that assume a premillennial interpretation of the end times, but it is also commonly found among those who claim to have no position with regard to the literal interpretation of John's account in Revelation of the end of the world. In practice, evangelicals of a variety of theological stripes have lived as though the world were a sinking ship. Polishing the brass or rearranging the deck chairs may be at best a kind of folly, at worst a tampering with God's unfathomable purposes. From this perspective, those who look to apply the teachings of Jesus to social, political, or economic questions dally with a "social gospel" that wrongly seeks to establish God's heavenly kingdom on earth.

The Spiritual Kingdom

A second and related idea in evangelical teaching equates the kingdom with a spiritual realm. This is an alternative idea to the future kingdom, though certainly not a contradictory one. Some of the great Christian thinkers have perpetuated the idea, none more so than Augustine, whose separation of humanity into a "city of God" and "city of man" has lived on as a highly influential Christian teaching. A close reading of his *City of God* casts doubt on the simple distinction that has been drawn from it; be that as it may, Augustine distinguished two "cities," one containing the saved, the other the unsaved, the former spiritual, the latter carnal or worldly and under the thrall of Satan. In the hands of many preachers, this view has bred a curious dualism in which care for the human soul coexists with indifference toward the entire created order. The theology of Christian responsibility that emerges from this teaching is sharply restricted to proclamation of the gospel, to a call to personal repentance and redemption. Social concerns might not be neglected altogether, but personal salvation is the paramount concern. Moreover, God redeems sinners, not governments or social welfare programs, and his redemptive acts do not extend to such institutions or programs. This world, carnal and rebellious, is passing away as God's justice is done and his kingdom comes. Redemption reaches only to the individual, not to the entire created order.

The Ambiguous Kingdom

Third, the idea of the kingdom of God is seen by many evangelicals as an ambiguous concept. Christians should place their faith in Jesus the Christ, not in some murky notion of a kingdom. We sense that this is the fallback position for the majority of evangelical pastors and lay persons who tend to consider sermons on the kingdom best left to liberal, mainline pastors pushing political agendas. Authentic biblical teaching, this view holds, centers on the Epistles of Paul or on Old Testament themes of God's judgment and forgiveness. It is hard to make much sense of the teachings on the kingdom. They don't speak to us as plainly as a well-crafted sermon on salvation by faith or the dangers of works. Miracles and parables refuse to fit neatly into such categories. So if neatness and fundamentals are at a premium, teaching on the kingdom will not feature prominently in a preacher's repertoire.

Each of these interpretations of the kingdom of Christ is deeply flawed. The strictly future kingdom, argue its critics, leads to one of two responses: total separation from one's culture or uncritical embrace of culture, society, and politics. Sociologist Robert Bellah observes that this line of thinking leads to a withdrawal into a kind of spiritual cell, seeking refuge and therapy in the local church. Church historian Martin Marty depicts embattled evangelicals either constructing a net of authority to fall back on or growing a shell of authority to provide protection from an onslaught of doubt and relativism. Conversely, James Hunter notes a simple accommodation of faith with culture, establishing in effect a kind of lifestyle model of evangelism that takes its cues from the culture's dominant norms.[1] Christianity remains distinctive to the nonbeliever only inasmuch as it offers a personal relationship with Jesus Christ while continuing to affirm the full benefits of the fun-filled, pleasure-seeking, wealth-oriented culture.

To affirm an exclusively spiritual kingdom is no less problematic. It denies in practice the sovereignty of God over all of his creation. If God is Lord of the heavens, he is certainly Lord of the earth as well. We take seriously the notion of a creation mandate by which humans have been called to be creators of culture. God is sovereign over the affairs of persons and governments; and precisely because he is sovereign, we should acknowledge his sovereignty in all aspects of human endeavor, including politics. A curiously truncated gospel is the accompaniment to a spiritualized version of the kingdom teachings.

Finally, to deny altogether the centrality of the teachings on the kingdom on the grounds of ambiguity is to insist that convenience or utility ought to be the foundation of the Christian message. Neither this objection nor its companion complaint that "liberals" may have co-opted the kingdom metaphor for their own political agendas can bear scrutiny. Indeed, we regard this as the most troubling of all responses because it forecloses examination of the central teachings of Jesus. We may surely call them central. Jesus almost always spoke in parables when he taught (Matt. 13:3, 34–35). And even if the teachings that are recorded in the Scriptures are a fraction of Jesus' teachings, it would be a very odd approach to Scripture to assume that they could be set aside when they occupy such a prominent place in his recorded sayings. For evangelicals especially, the traditional commitment to the Bible's authority ought to command attention proportionate to emphasis.

At this point you may be wondering to yourself, Okay, I can understand these objections. I even agree with them. But when will the authors get to their point? Just what are these kingdom teachings we must take so seriously in order to grasp the fullness of the gospel and its applicability to all of life? So far, the evangelical ship seems to have been scuttled; presumably it needs to be refitted. Where are the promised maps to help us chart our course for the missionary voyage into culture, society, and politics?

The Lord's Prayer is a helpful place to begin.

The Reality of the Kingdom

How should we pray? That question invites Jesus to outline the archetypal prayer, the elemental human response to the Creator-Redeemer God (Matt. 6:9–13; Luke 11:2–4). The Lord's Prayer witnesses to reality, it calls us to obedience to that reality and, in full recognition of human sinfulness, it lays down norms by which God's redemptive purposes for the whole creation may be realized.

Jesus' declaration of a new focus on what is real and true—God's kingdom—calls us to live oriented toward the kingdom and not to be guided by the counterfeit lodestar by which the world lives. In no sense, however, does the Lord's Prayer permit, much less encourage, a retreat from the world. Far from it. We are to pray for physical sustenance, forgiveness, and protection from evil. And *we* are to pray. The Lord's Prayer is not a means by which *I* seek special privileges from almighty God. Instead *we* link ourselves to one another to find true and fruitful fellowship, Christian to Christian, neighbor to neighbor. The Lord's Prayer confronts a false reality by which we distort our physical needs, pursue self-interest at the expense of the common good, and succumb to the author of lies. The Lord's Prayer is a prayer of truth versus falsehood, of love against hate, of ultimate reality against its imitators.

In the passages that follow in chapters 6–10, Matthew sustains his view of the universal scope and character of Jesus' teaching. The divine-human relationship that embraces personal conduct also reaches far beyond that conduct to our collective responsibility for human relationships, the care of creation, and the dimensions of spiritual warfare. Such a broad scope challenges the pietistic traditions so deeply ingrained in many of our evangelical churches, traditions that are inclined to represent all matters, private or public, as questions of personal conduct and ethics. Jesus' teachings on the kingdom do indeed address holiness, but it is a holiness that is as much corporate as it is personal. Jesus' teachings interpret the law, a law that Jesus himself summarized as the command to love God above oneself and to love one's neighbor as oneself (Matt. 22:37–40).

The Scope of the Kingdom

The first group of Jesus' teachings on the kingdom concerns personal conduct. With regard to fasting and earthly treasures (Matt. 6:16–24), Jesus calls his disciples to a modesty befitting the reality of the kingdom: No person can serve two masters. Verses 25–34 then challenge the disciples to "seek first his kingdom and his righteousness" rather than pursue the counterfeit reality dictated by the age we live in. We are not simply called to be faithful followers of Christ; we are promised emancipation from counterfeit reality to enter a relationship with God in which his provision extends even to the daily necessities of food and clothing. This is the challenge and the glory of radical commitment to faith in Christ. We are to live out that commitment in a world that encourages us to worry about a reality that has nothing to do with God's kingdom.

A second group of illustrations found in Matthew 7 and 8 concerns relations with others. Here, too, the context is the kingdom. Jesus teaches the disciples to take stock of the human condition and to count the cost of discipleship. Thus he warns in 7:6, "Do not give dogs what is holy." The world will seek to trample the truth of God's kingdom. So, too, while inviting his disciples to ask for the truth of his kingdom (7:7–12), he prepares them for more than just a personal commitment to himself. Wisdom (7:15–29), faith (8:1–17, 23–27), and counting the cost (7:18–22) are the minimum personal attributes that the kingdom requires.

In chapter 9, Matthew illustrates the difference between living by kingdom standards and living by worldly standards in accounts of the healing of the paralytic, the calling of Matthew, and Jesus' response to questions from John the Baptist's disciples about fasting. The Pharisees, working from within their own pietistic and legalistic framework, condemn Jesus' forgiveness of the paralytic as blasphemy, but Jesus' response demonstrates his authority as the Son of God—he heals the paralytic. The result? The crowd who sees this praises God. We are left to consider what the response of the teachers of the law might have been. Amazement? Embarrassment? Anger? Matthew's account does not say. But we are invited to reflect on Jesus' willingness to go beyond what the conventional religion of the day would have either expected or called for. In radical fulfillment of the Mosaic law, Jesus demonstrates that forgiveness not only supersedes but also precedes healing. In verses 9–13, the calling of the tax collector Matthew, we gain further perspective on the scope of God's kingdom. Again, the Pharisees voice suspicion: Why would Jesus associate with someone as vile as a tax collector? Jesus' response (vv. 12–13) underscores the good news that the kingdom is indeed in and for the world. "Those who are well have no need of a physician, but those who are sick. . . . For I came not to call the righteous, but sinners."

The kingdom depicted in these passages encompasses God's norms for every sphere of life—personal conduct, social and political relations, and the care of the created order itself.

The Parables of the Kingdom

"Kingdom" has two related meanings. As we have employed it so far, it refers to the domain over which the king reigns—the physical realm. But the New Testament word *basilea* may also be rendered as the exercise of the king's power. In *The Parables of the Kingdom,* Robert Farrar Capon finds Jesus' parables to be parables of power. But what a strangely paradoxical power it is! The kingdom proclaimed by Jesus, Capon warns, defies "the 'right-handed' logicalities of theology" by favoring "the 'left-handed' mystery of faith."[2] And, of course, once he has said that, we begin to remember Jesus' mysterious warning that the kingdom could be entered only with the faith of little children (Matt. 18:3). We see both faith and power in God's seemingly careless scattering of the Word to fall where it will in the world (Matt. 13:1–9); in the wheat left to grow along with the all-but-identical, yet counterfeit, weeds (13:24–30); in the invisible but active leaven (13:33); and in the all-encompassing net, gathering in good, bad, and indifferent alike (13:47–50). Here is the kingdom as the Word of God sown in the world like seed and, like seed, "forgotten"—left to do its own work.

For Capon, the "left-handed" faithful character of God's exercise of kingship manifests itself in summary principles that are fully consistent with our sketch of the kingdom's norms, which we derived from treating "kingdom" in the spatial sense of a domain or realm. The healings and teachings of Jesus, as well as the Lord's Prayer, assert the present reality and universal scope of the kingdom; the parables attest to its power in the world and its catholicity. In Capon's words, Jesus insists that the kingdom is at work "everywhere, always, and for all, rather than in some places, at some times, for some people."[3] When Jesus sketches his parabolic characters or circumstances, he drafts them so inclusively that no one, at any time or in any place, is left outside the scope of his teaching. It may be the rich man and Lazarus, or the characters in the parable of the Good Samaritan, or the lost sheep or the net—each of us is drawn to the parables as proper object of their teachings.

Capon goes on to remind us that the Word is accorded a hostile reception more often than not; antagonism and indifference are soils every bit as common as receptiveness.[4] But the resurrection of Christ has already overcome the power of Satan. Like unwitting birds who participate in the propagation of plants by swallowing their fruits and voiding their seeds, the devil may devour the good works of the kingdom, but the Word will survive unscathed.

The indelible impression left by the parables of the kingdom is one of catholicity, mystery, and power. The parables deserve much more attention than we have given them; yet even from this cursory examination it is evident that they confirm the perspective suggested above—a kingdom found growing in the world, not apart from it. Not a strictly future kingdom, nor an exclusively spiritual kingdom, the kingdom of heaven is the realm of God's rule in power even if the mystery of its operation defies the simple cause-effect, means-ends logic we would apply to it.

The Kingdom and Politics

In these opening chapters we have tried to equip
Christians with compass and map. Chapter 1 pictured
the believer as a sojourner-citizen and argued that both
aspects direct us to responsible, insightful, and critical
public service. In this chapter we have reinforced and
extended that perspective by examining Jesus' prayers,
teachings, and parables concerning the kingdom of
God. Four main lessons can be derived from the New
Testament treatment of the kingdom. First, the kingdom is a present reality. Its fullness, its completion, and
its glorification await the end of the age, but the Word
sown and growing in the world is truly the kingdom.
This is the good news that Christians should declare to
the fallen reality of the culture, society, and world in
which we live, to neighbor and nation alike. Second,
the kingdom calls us to a loyalty grounded in faith and
exercised in obedience to Jesus Christ. To apprehend
the reality of the kingdom cannot be an intellectual exercise alone but must include a radical commitment to
its Lord. Third, the ethics of the kingdom must be carefully identified and consciously applied in the witness
of the church. In particular, evangelicals should resist
the tendency to reduce them to a purely personal ethics.
Fourth, Christians are called to believe, to put their trust
in the one whose love is a powerful agent, the yeast in
the dough of the fallen world. Our every act should be
done out of God's love.

Surprisingly, our response to the kingdom can and
should be a simple one. From the parable of the sower
Capon draws the conclusion that Christians are called
to bear good fruit, not to accomplish good works. Good
works are the fruit of the kingdom (Col. 1:10), among
which the writer of Hebrews commends in particular

"the peaceful fruit of righteousness" (Heb. 12:11), the foundation for harmonious personal relationships and a just society alike. To fail to produce fruit is to risk losing the kingdom, Jesus warned the Jews, placing fruitfulness definitively above claims of status or history (Matt. 21:43). No wonder the disciples pressed Jesus so persistently about how to attain salvation. Jesus' reply, "Only believe" (John 5:24), takes us all by surprise with its simplicity.

Up to this point, we have dealt only indirectly with the implications of the kingdom for government, concentrating instead on the kingdom as a vehicle for confronting Christians with the reality and scale of the gospel, and thus with the scope of their responsibilities and the resources with which to meet them. But that is only half the equation, as understanding the kingdom sheds light not only on our responsibilities but on their object.

Political authority, be it democratic or autocratic, is routinely associated with the exercise of lawful power. To link it to love would be remarkable and would get short shrift from political scientists. God's kingship connotes legal and governmental status, as we have seen, whether kingship refers to the exercise of authority or to the domain within which the king exercises it. But God's kingdom is an order of existence entered by faith and characterized by love. Love is expressed in righteousness and justice. Hence the kingdom casts law and government principally as expressions of love, and only secondarily as manifestations of power. Power is ancillary, necessary, of course, but its exercise conforms to love. In this way, love and politics are reconnected and the mystery of love's place in politics is solved.

Down through the centuries, Augustine's warning to Cicero that "true justice is not of this world" has gone unheeded—or has become the root of an unhealthy dualism of which the expedient power politics of Machi-

avelli is the logical outcome. Love has long been sup-
planted by power in political analyses, yet politics requires the kingdom. Coercion (raw power) never yields
the "peaceful fruit of righteousness." Machiavelli's
Prince, a "textbook" on getting and keeping power, presents an unstable, suspicion-ridden dynamic as the description of the never-ending scramble to stay at the
top of the power pyramid. Power politics is built with
very limited resources. Equipped only with military
force, strategic sense, and cunning, Machiavelli's anti-
hero projects a reality that is their reflection. Small wonder that he concedes to Fortune half of life's outcomes!
Nor is power politics poor in resources alone. Without
trust and love, it tries to create a new order of existence
by making auxiliary implements do the work of primary ones. The result is an order in which power is
unchecked and justice—giving to each his or her due—
remains unattainable.

We do not characterize all politics as out-and-out
Machiavellian. Political systems display varying degrees
of concern for justice. But if Christians are to take their
bearings from the kingdom, we must appreciate the part
played by kingdom principles in government, as well
as the perils of their exclusion. The kingdom is vital to
a Christian understanding of politics both because it
describes reality and prescribes our response to it and
because it sheds the light of that reality on the political order.

With map and compass in hand, we may now turn
our attention to the vessel in which we will sail—it is
time to examine churches and the church, visible and
invisible. With the help of Scripture, we shall consider
what God intends the church to be. With the help of
church history and the American Constitution, we shall
examine the forms it has actually taken.

STUDY QUESTIONS

1. How have you understood Jesus' teachings on the kingdom? Which of the teachings do you identify with most closely? Why?
2. What do the authors mean by the "reality" of the kingdom? What practical difference might this perspective make for your life in Christ?
3. The authors argue that the scope of the kingdom embraces public responsibility as well as personal evangelism and discipleship. Do you agree? How does their view affect the way you read, understand, and apply the gospel?
4. The authors describe the Lord's Prayer as presenting a summary of kingdom principles: The reality of the kingdom declared in the prayer calls forth a corresponding loyalty and ethics. Do you agree with this interpretation of the prayer? How might this interpretation influence the teaching, worship, and outreach of your church?
5. How do Jesus' parables of the kingdom (Matt. 13) illuminate your understanding of the kingdom?
6. In what ways are love and trust foundational to political and other public relationships (whether described as Christian/kingdom principles or not)?

3

Setting Sail in the Church

"The church" is the body of Christ (1 Cor. 12:27), a Spirit-filled community (2 Cor. 3:6–18), and a place where God lives by his Spirit (Eph. 2:22). In the apostles and Old Testament prophets it has historical foundations, and its basic foundation is Jesus Christ himself (Eph. 2:20). The Greek word *ekklesia* means "called out," and the church, whom Paul describes as "fellow citizens with the saints and members of the household of God" (Eph. 2:19), earns this by becoming resident aliens in the world—that is, sojourners, as we discussed in the first chapter. What is striking about these passages is that they describe the church in flesh-and-blood terms, in terms inescapably worldly. While the church is clearly a community of the Spirit—God's Holy Spirit, after all, lives in it—it does not assume an otherworldly character. Instead, its center, no less than the incarnation of Christ, is here on earth. As to its completion or perfec-

43

tion, that indeed awaits the end of the age, when the powers and principalities that have fought against Christ will be suppressed (Rev. 20). But as Robert Webber puts it so well, the church "is a spiritual reality *in the world* [italics ours] that unfolds within the order of existence and participates in salvation history."[1]

The church is a dwelling place of God in the Spirit. Paul's choice of words may cause momentary confusion, inviting images of soaring Gothic cathedrals containing somehow the Holy Spirit of God. But the dwelling place Paul describes is people, not buildings. For *we* are the church, the *laos,* or people, of God. And if we *are* the church, then we should beg off a language that suggests we only go *to* church on Sundays or for weeknight Bible studies or potluck suppers. The sole geographic designation admitted by the early church identified the local congregations by the name òf the towns in which they were to be found, such as "God's people at Corinth"—or Ephesus or Wichita or Garden Grove.

This leads directly to our next point. If the church is a spiritual reality in the world that unfolds within the order of existence and participates in salvation history, then, in Webber's words again, "the church is more than an association of believers or an institution established by Jesus."[2] No, the church is even described as participating in the work of Christ in the world, becoming the "fulness" of Christ (Eph. 1:23). The emphasis, then, is not on our joining—that is, assenting or believing—but on our participating in the history of redemption and judgment. Significantly, the terms used to describe the church evoke relationships and functions quite different from the bonds and roles evoked by beliefs. We are called family members, and what family is held together primarily by common beliefs? To be a family member is also to have a variety of household tasks to perform, so that family life may run smoothly. As for the status "citizen," which we addressed in the previous chapter, citizenship confers both rights and responsibilities. Aristotle used the term to refer to one whose social standing required him to participate in the community's administration. Here, then, are images of the church quite at odds with the concept of a "belief group."

Belief has a vital role in the life of the church, but we wonder whether the disciples gave the world an example of *belief*—assent to various propositions—or of *faith*—a partly responsible, partly reckless response to Jesus' invitation to follow him. Belief of the first sort has become so much a part of the life of the church, especially among Protestant denominations, that we may perhaps lose sight of the fact that biblical callings out to true faith—whether of Abram to leave home and culture or of the disciples to become fishers of men—served to distinguish the church from those who did not follow. Time and time again, disputes over "belief" have resulted in the fracturing of the body of Christ.

It is not our purpose here to make sweeping claims about the validity of the splits and schisms that have affected Christianity from the earliest times. Our aim is to show that we, the church, have been called out from the world by Jesus Christ to take part in his redemptive work in the world. We are not to think of faith primarily as the glue that unifies the church or to think of our local congregations as belief groups. As to the church's unity, Paul is quite clear: Christ is the head of the body (Col. 1:18). As for our local congregations, centuries of doctrinal, liturgical, theological, and social divergence notwithstanding, we remain simply "those at Laodicea," "the saints and faithful brethren at Colossae," "the church of God which is at Corinth," or even "the church in your house" (Philem. 1:2).

The Ministry of the Laity

We could take several approaches to examining the vessel that is the church in the world. What we intend to do is to discuss the practical implications of the biblical vision of the church we have presented. To do this, we compare the biblical church with the American churches in order to make a series of recommendations for local congregations. The burden of the negative side of our argument is that the church in the United States has taken on forms that bear only slight resemblance to the real, biblical church. Nautically speaking, most churches resemble houseboats anchored in secluded coves; the New Testament reality is more like a schooner with oceangoing capabilities. Since we have begun with a biblical argument, however, let's stay with it for the present and postpone the sociological, historical, and political discussion of existing churches until later in the chapter.

You feed a body for the work it is to do. As members of the body of Christ, we need nourishment fitting for our work in the world. The organization, administration, and teaching ministries of our churches are a vital source of this nourishment, but they are a means to an end, not the end itself. The organization (clergy, staff, physical plant) are established to serve the life of the body from which they spring. How unfortunate that they should, in so many cases, have taken on the very title "church" and controlled the meaning of what it is to be the church. This is an all-too-familiar pattern. Whether it be politics, business, or churches, organizations are forever worrying about themselves rather than the purposes for which they were created.

Here, too, we must resist the temptation to digress. Our point is simply that the ministry of the church is the ministry of the laity, the people, the whole body of Christ. It is not solely the ministry of the clergy, or of the services and programs that represent the organization "in action." No, the clergy are themselves called out, from the laity, to serve the body of Christ in certain special capacities as preachers and teachers, pastors and priests, to serve by "serving up" the food that nourishes the body of Christ. The special status of the clergy has no other legitimate sources than these. It is to the credit of traditions like the Pentecostals that they have worked to preserve this aspect of the New Testament church.

Of course, our work in the world includes worship, for we are to love God first and foremost and wholeheartedly. But the second commandment is "like unto it." Loving our neighbor as ourselves encompasses at least raising children, teaching, administration, political representation, designing systems to improve the quality of life, and finding ways to reduce the harm we do to one another from our multifarious activities. The second commandment calls for at least as careful instruction and encouragement as the first if we are to do all these things well. Do we receive such instruction and encouragement from the pulpit and in the Sunday school class?

The Church in the United States

A well-recognized distinction between the *church* and the *sect* clarifies the organization of congregations from the early church to the present. The sect stood apart from society, typically organized itself in egalitarian fashion, and earnestly awaited the return of Christ. Perhaps it was largely because they expected Jesus' imminent return that these Christians paid relatively little attention to crafting organizations that would survive for the long haul. In contrast, other Christians began to think that the church needed to address questions about a future in which Christ's second coming did not figure prominently. They were disposed to plan ahead, to ask about ways to preserve Christ's teachings, to organize evangelism, and to regularize relations with the governing authorities. Of even greater significance was the attention they paid to governing themselves. In time, their forms and styles and rubrics came almost to define the faith. In response, various sects formed periodically, usually inspired by a suspicion that the organized church really wasn't the biblical church any more: It was too close and cozy with the status quo, it stifled various freedoms and religious practices, it failed to serve the poor, its structures were unscriptural. Paradoxically, but hardly surprisingly, the sects in turn developed their own traditions, customs, and rubrics and risked sectarian challenges of their own.

In the United States, sects flourished—and continue to do so—but they were so free to prosper that they took on many of the organizational features of churches. Conversely, churches (Roman Catholic, Anglican, and Lutheran, for example) faced considerable pressure to take on certain sectlike characteristics, stressing and often bending to their local congregations, accepting a good deal more democracy in their congregational government than was traditional. At the same time, the presence of a large number of religious traditions helped to give both church and sect a common identity: the denomination.

The denomination is not a uniquely American form, although the United States may claim to have given it its decisive shape. Denominations accept a relational definition. Instead of each claiming the title of church, they settle for a definition that amounts to belief group. Their distinguishing characteristic is one that must distinguish them from other bodies of Christians, not one that will describe their relationship to God and to the world. Belief is that characteristic. It may be a belief expressed as loyalty to a greater or lesser theologian (e.g., Lutherans, Campbellites), or belief expressed in a particular form of self-government (e.g., Presbyterians, Episcopalians), or belief reflective of a doctrinal emphasis (e.g., Adventists, Pentecostals, Baptists). The denomination resolved the presence of other traditions by giving up the biblical status of the church (the body of Christ), which was consequently to lodge nowhere in American Christianity except perhaps in the Roman Catholic Church or among the much smaller numbers of Orthodox Christians. In exchange, denominational religion received a high degree of legitimacy and social acceptability and enjoyed wide-ranging freedom—including the freedom to splinter into new denominations or to merge with old ones. Even those denominations with traditions as churches rather than sects, such as the Episcopalians, have availed themselves of the freedom to splinter on the grounds of belief.[3]

And so church history has brought us to the same conclusion we reached with the assistance of theology: The American church has adopted very largely a form that is ill suited to function as Christ's body in the world.

Religion and the American Constitution

The concern about the voluntary privatization of the American church is compounded by the public definition of religion that is now dominant in America. The church defines itself as a private belief group; the Amer-

ican Constitution reinforces this definition by bestow-
ing public approval on it and public disapproval on de-
viant forms and practices.

It is not easy to see this at first glance. The usual response to the separation of church and state is to argue
that it fosters a breadth of religious liberty without parallel in the world. Indeed, the flowering of religious diversity in the United States testifies to the prodigious
scope of that liberty. American religious liberty has been
and continues to be a precious thing, but those First
Amendment freedoms warrant a second look.

The Constitution has little to say about religion. The
original document—the one signed by the delegates to
the Philadelphia Convention of 1787—made one short
reference to religion: No religious test could be imposed
as a qualification for holding an office under government of the United States (Article VI, Section 3). There's
not much that can be read into this. Indeed, historian
John Wilson has suggested that it is best understood in
its political frame of reference. In Wilson's view, the
framers saw religious diversity as a political problem—
it threatened the national unity they hoped to secure
for the new republic they were founding—so they attempted to remove its potential for conflict. By forbid-
ding religious tests for holding office, they removed a
religious set of grounds for refusing to support the new
Constitution.

The Bill of Rights, made up of ten amendments addressing primarily individual liberties, was incorporated
into the Constitution in 1791. The first of these amendments sets forth religious liberty along with freedom of
speech, press, and assembly. Here, too, the Constitution's treatment is notable for its brevity: "Congress
shall make no law respecting an establishment of religion or prohibiting the free exercise thereof." We would
probably be wise to follow Wilson's advice again and

not overinterpret, for here again the context is political, not religious. The First Amendment religion clauses do not explain what "religion" is. "Religion" simply helps to interpret the relationship between individuals and the government. It is considered an individual right of central importance and is supplied with near-absolute protection against the intrusion of government. The two clauses referring to religion are complementary. We could paraphrase them to say, "Because religion is a basic human right, the federal government may neither make a person conform to a particular, official practice of it nor prevent its practice by any person."

The Constitution may reflect the framers' views of religion well; it may reflect them poorly. It is hard to tell. But the consequences of the treatment they gave it are significant far beyond that question. For by insisting that freedom of religion is among the foundational *individual* rights (and being otherwise silent on the substance of religion), the framers effectively restricted the definition of religion to liberty of conscience. Religion is fundamentally personal, not found in groups or communities except insofar as individuals construct them. It is an individual thing, a private thing, something that goes on in one's head.

From this point of view, a conception of the church as the body of Christ receives no support in the Constitution. By extension from the First Amendment treatment of religion, churches came to be defined for the most part as groups of people whose personal beliefs coincided. If religion is to be found in the intimate wrestling with one's conscience, the church that the Constitution protects is one that projects the same essentially private and voluntary characteristics. Religious diversity represents nothing more than the distinct patterns that personal beliefs exhibit. Churches are voluntary associations of believers: belief groups. Whatever happened to the body of Christ?

The history of the religion clauses of the Constitution is vast and intricate. Suffice it to say, however, that the restricted definition of religion afforded by its treatment in the Constitution is congenial to a strict separation of church and state. The "wall of separation" (Jefferson's expression coined in a letter to a friend and not, as some mistakenly assume, a part of the Constitution) was to be built high and thick to *protect* religious liberty. Keeping government out would benefit individuals and churches no less than it would free government from particular religious influences. This is pretty harmless—*as long as you can go along with the restricted definition of religion*. But consider again the New Testament view of the church as Christ's body. From its perspective, the separation of church and state presents a formidable obstacle to the essentially public life of that body.

The upshot is this: Americans enjoy near-absolute liberty of conscience or private religious belief. No state-run church can extract obedience from them, let alone dollars to pay for its upkeep. But let the churches leave the private (or charitable) domains the Constitution accepts as legitimate or let them enter a public dispute, and they run into a wall of constraints. Strikingly reflective of these is a semantic about-face. In their private activities, government is quite willing to call them "churches." Let them take a public posture, however, and they immediately become "sects"—an ironic misunderstanding if ever there was one![4]

Born of these constraints is an attitude shared by Christian and non-Christian alike in the United States, that the separation of church and state entails a separation of religion from politics. We point this out not to go over the familiar contradictions in this view (for religion and politics have always been intertwined in American history and American political theory) but to note with regret the way in which the privatization of religion is reinforced by such an attitude. The resultant sacred-secular dualism further encourages an attitude of suspicion on the part of Christians toward politics every bit the equal of official suspicion of "sectarian" public activity.

These handicaps hinder the effectiveness of American churches and raise serious doubts as to the scope of religious liberty in the United States. Christians might profit from examining the theological underpinnings of all of this, for in the spirit of our metaphor, the American church is not seaworthy because its owners haven't tried to purchase the necessary parts—but as we can now see, even if they did try, the government wouldn't sell them.

Church and Kingdom

This handbook on politics has taken up three chapters without getting close to the subject, or so it must seem. You may have decided that the authors have all but torpedoed the entire project by declaring the American churches unfit for a public role in which they will certainly be unwelcome. If that thought has gone through your minds, we can only admit that it often goes through ours. But we think it's better to face up to that possibility than to ignore it. And if it helps, all the shipwrecks in Scripture turn out to be resurrection stories.

The task that we face is no less comprehensive than the one set forth in the previous chapter on the teachings on the kingdom. There we argued that those teachings call us to treat the kingdom, sown and growing in the world, as a present reality from which to take our bearings as Christians. To do so requires a loyalty to Jesus Christ manifested in faith and obedience, and an ethics proportionate to the universal reach of God's sovereign power and love.

Kingdom and church go hand in hand. A biblical view of the church naturally complements that of the kingdom, for in the church, the followers of Jesus declare the good news of the kingdom sown in the world. The form the Bible ascribes to the church reflects the this-worldliness, catholicity, and power of the kingdom: It is at work in the world, it is open to all, and it manifests itself in what the world can only call weakness. The forms that churches have taken, by their own choice and under political constraints, fail the standard of this biblical vision of kingdom and church when they retreat from the world, when they emphasize exclusion rather than inclusion, and when they borrow the world's strong-arm tactics in their infrequent forays into the political arena.

We find ourselves calling for nothing less than a revolution in lay thinking about the proper "location" of the church, one that will also call on our clergy to reappraise their ministries and recapture along with the laity the vision of the early church, which set aside special offices for service, never thinking for a moment that those offices should usurp the title and identity of the church itself.

You may be thinking that a revolution is going a bit too far and isn't very practical. Revolutions are not everyday occurrences, after all. But a revolution is practical precisely in the sense that it gets back to the reality of the Christian faith. You cannot make a silk purse from a sow's ear, as the old saying goes. Practicality always begins with the facts and works out from them. And the facts about the church are to be found in biblical descriptions of it rather than in the adaptations wrought by churches in response to social and political circumstances. The revolution we are calling for need not be a large-scale housecleaning, however. It's a marvelous truth about Christianity that from its inception, a small group of unlikely individuals embodied the risen Christ and became, beyond their wildest expectations, his healing hands, his compassionate arms, and his feet shod with the gospel of peace. The small group or the Sunday school class is an excellent setting in which to explore the questions of biblical interpretation raised here.

We recommend a small-scale approach for another reason. We are convinced that most attempts to teach politics in the churches break up on ideological reefs. To seek Christian unity on political or ideological grounds is to make exactly the same mistake made by churches that fashioned themselves as belief groups and thereafter split early and often. Only when members of congregations have discussed and owned a New Testament view of the church for themselves is discussion of political responsibility likely to bear good fruit. Being sent out into the world as Christ's hands, arms, and feet is more a question of having faith in Jesus who sends us than of insisting on common doctrinal positions on the right way to heal, to love, or to do justice.

STUDY QUESTIONS

1. Do you agree with the biblical view of the church presented here? Have the authors adopted too broad or too narrow a view of the church?

2. In what ways does your own congregation reflect
   the theology of the church described here? How
   does it depart from that theology? Why may this
   have happened?
3. Is the authors' distinction between the church as
   the body of Christ and the church as belief group
   a valid distinction in practice? Must churches
   sometimes choose between a theological ideal on
   the one hand and preservation of biblical teaching on the other?
4. How do you respond to the authors' reading of
   the American Constitution's treatment of religion?
   Must the consequences be as bleak for the church
   as the authors allege?
5. How might the practical steps toward a recovery
   of the church, as set out here, be implemented in
   your congregation? What format would be most
   appropriate? Do your denomination's traditions
   raise any obstacles to pursuing the kind of study
   recommended in the text?

4

Beyond Piecemeal Politics

I n the first three chapters, we have tried to show that a Christian approach to politics must begin with what God reveals—what the Bible teaches—about who we are and about the unfolding drama in which we play a part. More prosaically, we must start with the Bible's teaching on persons, on the kingdom, and on the church. On the basis of these teachings we have represented the individual person as a "sojourner-citizen"; we have found in the image of the kingdom the sovereign power and love of God at work in the whole created order, not just in believers or groups of believers alone; and we have presented the body of Christ in the world as the New Testament conception of the church.

Our purpose in this chapter is to show how this theological reorientation can lead local congregations toward their public responsibilities naturally—that is, without an artificial leap into Christian politics. Unbeknown to many parishioners, an important source of political ideas lies in their own congregations. This source is simply their common life as members of the body of Christ.

Piecemeal Politics Revisited

Let us first review our analysis of the defective approach to public responsibility we have termed "piecemeal politics." We have used the term to describe the issue-by-issue approach to public life so common among evangelical Christians. To make our point again, that approach permits a definition of Christian political activity as something temporary or unnatural to be smuggled into our thinking unseen and unquestioned. Once such a definition has made its home in our consciousness, it effectively closes the door to a truly comprehensive Christian approach to public life. Having no vocabulary of its own to describe political issues, piecemeal politics leaves Christians floundering in the public square either as rank amateurs devoid of worldly wisdom or as uncritical wielders of political tools and techniques fashioned by others, or even as supplicants for the satisfaction of church interests. Intent as it is on quick reforms, piecemeal politics never sticks around long enough to develop the principles necessary for a permanent Christian presence in government. We need Christian principles for lawmaking and administration, not for reform only.

In the first three chapters we attempted to uncover the basic weaknesses of piecemeal politics in greater detail: deficiencies in theology regarding the kingdom and the church, restrictions imposed by the privatized denominational form of the church in North America, and constraints stemming from church-state separation in the United States. We would add two further concerns. First, piecemeal politics does not regard relationships within the church as having much to do with those in the wider world. The theological roots of piecemeal politics lie in dualistic teachings on the kingdom that either separate this world from a strictly future kingdom or distinguish so sharply between carnal and spiritual that the latter has little to say to the former. This sort of perspective is unlikely to encourage the view that the local congregation may be a nursery for growing biblical principles directed to public justice in the wider world.

Parables and Principles

On the positive side, simply identifying piecemeal politics with all its attendant problems makes it easier to move beyond that sort of approach to something better. The reorientation in biblical perspective of chapters 1 through 3 has immediate practical application: It can lower barriers raised by privatization, spiritualization of kingdom teachings, and denominationalism. And if it can do that, it can also pave the way for transforming the most important relationships in which Christians live their lives: between members of churches, between the church and the world, between local congregations and the communities in which they are situated, and among local congregations of different denominations. This new perspective can also help us improve our individual and corporate relationships with the living God.

We think, too, that the process we describe is in keeping with the way Jesus taught. He taught in parables,

and parables invite us to go away and ponder their mes-
sages in everyday situations. Unlike much prescriptive
teaching, which can be fixed, wooden, and lifeless, the
pedagogy of the parables is alive, their lessons unfolding along with the narrative. A parable is a gracious form
of teaching whose obliqueness does not force us into
direct confrontation with its moral prescriptions until
we are prepared to receive them. Above all, the parables
convey living principles, and Christians will never devise sound policies unless they have first owned the
principles that lie beneath them. The parables contra-
dict treatment of the Bible as a cookbook of recipes for
every contingency, a treatment that strangles its message of undeserved love and calls into question its capacity to respond to a world that has left the first century A.D. far behind. Jesus made no attempt to prescribe
static solutions to the entire range of potential issues
and situations. Indeed, it is questionable whether he
ever offered the first century A.D. anything that could
be described as policy. Asked how individuals should
act or whether specific laws were legitimate, Jesus took
his questioners back to principles: "What is the law?
You shall love the Lord your God and your neighbor as
yourself." Even seemingly concrete prescriptions that
smack of policy such as "render to Caesar" are statements of principle.

Complementing his teaching in parables, Jesus com-
mended expressions of faith throughout his earthly
ministry. Just as principles may be derived from God's
Word in the Scriptures that are his revelation to us, so
faith grounds us firmly in the reality of God's love and
the working of his kingdom in the world.

Why do the parables become so understandable and
memorable after we struggle to glean the teachings they
contain? Perhaps it is because this *method* of teaching
places its lessons within everyday stories: A farmer went

out to sow his seed; the kingdom of heaven is like trea-
sure hidden in a field; a man planted a vineyard; and
so on. And the morals, the principles that eventually
emerge from those everyday stories, retain their association with them, rooting their applications no less
firmly in daily life. This is why we argue that following
the spirit of Jesus' teaching is a matter not of orthodoxy
(right *teaching*) alone, but of teaching people in the right
place also. The right place to teach principles for public
life is in the congregation, as close as possible to the
daily lives of the people of God, and the location of the
very problems that need to be addressed. As we stressed
in chapter 3, this location must not foreclose, in teaching or organization, the kinds of conversations Christians must engage in if they are to develop the principles of public justice that underlie a Christian politics.

What we will do now is present several examples of
how to encourage the local congregation to become a
nursery for developing just political, social, and economic principles. We chose them not as success stories
but as representative Christian strategies. Together they
confirm the wisdom of a biblical theology of the church
and point to the importance of developing principles
within the congregation.

Example #1: Stewardship

All Saints' Episcopal Church in West Newbury, Massachusetts, decided to try an experiment in stewardship
in 1991. Over the years, the church's stewardship practices had been periodically overhauled as the congregation searched for a faithful way to reflect the Bible's
teaching on stewardship. For example, some years ago
in an attempt to place church budgeting on the basis
of faith, each household's pledge cards were collected

on the appointed Sunday and offered to God and then
burned so that the pledges were known only to the
members of that household. The pledges were recorded,
but the amount pledged by any person or family was
not known to anyone else in the church. Two things
were accomplished: The household emphasis of stewardship was reaffirmed, and the vestry were encouraged
to act on faith in planning how to serve the needs of
the congregation.

In 1991, the church went one step farther. Parishioners felt that the entire process still conveyed the
wrong message, a message that stewardship was still, at
root, concerned with running the church financially.
They asked how they could convey instead that the
church's role was to teach and serve the congregation
in their individual, familial, and corporate cultivation
of God's good creation.

In attempting to set matters on a more biblical foot-
ing, three sets of issues were distinguished: those sur-
rounding the Bible's teaching on stewardship; household money matters; and church budgetary issues. After
some discussion, the sets of issues were linked to one
another like this: The theology of the church as the
body of Christ (God's people in the world) led the
vestry/stewardship committee to see its task as serving
the needs of the members by good teaching on stewardship and by discussion, sharing, and advice regarding individual and family finances throughout the congregation. They instituted a program of discussion of
financial responsibility and planning, personal approaches, fears about money, conceptions of just financial management, debt forgiveness, materialism,
and a number of related issues.

Church budgeting was removed from its typically intimate linkage to stewardship so that the vestry and
clergy could first fulfill their office of bringing man and

God together on the issues. Only then were church bud-getary matters reintroduced to the discussion in their supplementary role of facilitating the work of the church (the people of God). During the experimental period, the church postponed "Pledge Sunday" until these other matters had been given priority.

All of this reorganization of traditional stewardship activities amounted to a course of instruction in and of itself. Its immediate consequences were as follows:

1. To remove the discussion from an *ecclesiastical* frame of reference.
2. To *democratize* the issue (as one involving a highly differentiated parish, made up of individuals, families, college students, the wealthy, the less wealthy, the retired, the unemployed, and so forth).
3. To *broaden the scope* of the issue as it would other-wise have been conceived, and thus to take the discussion well beyond the concerns of member families. This happened because to recognize their diversity was to take into account the other com-munities—local, state, professional, and so forth—to which they also belonged, together with the economic dynamics of those communities.

As a result, the church's discussion of economics be-came more, not less, of a Christian discussion because it grew out of and reinforced a better view of the church. Practically speaking, they had eliminated the artificial barrier between church and world, local congregation and local community. They had given substance to the belief that Christians are sojourner-citizens; teaching and service were to meet people where they lived their lives.

Thus the principles developed out of a consideration of stewardship have become for All Saints' Episcopal Church principles with wider application. The striking thing about the changes is how relatively small they were. It was not necessary to tear apart the fabric of church government to achieve them. Their impact promises to be far-reaching, however, because they have changed the environment in which stewardship questions are considered. At the very least, they have signaled a greater openness to members of the congregation to talk about household economics and to find the church listening; they can encourage us to bring the needs of the wider world into our thoughts, prayers, and deliberations.

Example #2: The Solitary Sojourner

Our second example features a crusader for justice, a solitary sojourner who took on the American government and lost, but in the process underwent a profound political education. Steve Comley is a farmer-businessman from Rowley, Massachusetts, where he owns and operates the Seaview Nursing Home. In the early 1980s, construction of a nuclear power plant in nearby Seabrook, New Hampshire (about twelve miles away), attracted nationwide attention. At the time, Steve Comley had no particular interest in politics or in the nuclear power industry. He did have a great concern, however, regarding the elderly people in his care. As discussions began in New Hampshire and Massachusetts regarding evacuation plans in the event of a nuclear accident at the plant, Mr. Comley soon realized that there was very little he could do to protect those people. He felt it was his duty to find out more.

In short order, Mr. Comley became embroiled in a controversy with the Nuclear Regulatory Commission (NRC) and the federal court system of the United States. During his research of the licensing process of the Seabrook plant, Mr. Comley met a member of the NRC staff who, together with other Seabrook employees, informed him that substandard materials and procedures had been used in its construction. Disturbed by what he had learned, Mr. Comley formed We the People, a citizens group that highlighted the problems at Seabrook and sought to provide protection to nuclear industry whistle-blowers who might have information relevant to the construction and operation of the nuclear power plants. In a political controversy that spilled over into the courts, Mr. Comley was ordered on safety grounds to turn over information that he was alleged to have received from these whistle-blowers. He refused, stating that the NRC was derelict in its duty to the public. At one time, besides several hundreds of thousands of dollars in fines, Mr. Comley faced the prospect of time in prison for refusing to turn over information the courts believed he had obtained illegally.

Seated at his desk in his office at Seaview Nursing Home—an office styled after the Oval Office in the White House—Mr. Comley explained to us the values that underlay his actions: "My experience as a student, farmer, and businessman has helped shape who I am. My parents [from whom he learned the nursing care business] taught me to take my responsibility to care for the elderly seriously. When I toured the Seabrook plant and found out that there was no possibility of evacuation in case of an accident, I felt that I owed it to my seniors to investigate more thoroughly."

He went on to share his deep commitment to grass-roots democracy. After personally delivering informa-

tion on Seabrook to President Reagan at a fund-raiser
(Mr. Comley is a lifelong Republican), his frustration
spilled over at the president's lack of response. "When
the president of the United States was ignoring the
people of Rowley [over 80 percent of the town had expressed opposition to the licensing of the Seabrook
plant], he has an obligation to listen to me, to not ignore me. So that's what really got me fired up. We live
in an open democracy in this country, and I expect my
people to be part of the solution. The more I was
shunned in Washington, the angrier I got."

Mr. Comley's convictions are informed by his faith.
"I feel the Lord is leading me. My faith works for me.
I'm not here to force people to believe in God. I am after
justice. I don't feel any vengeance toward the NRC. I
just want them to do their job, that's all."

As the struggle dragged on, Mr. Comley sought coun-
sel from Christian friends. His pastor at a local church
has continued to provide personal and spiritual coun-
sel. Yet few Christians have lent active support. In part,
this is because the battle is largely a legal one now. But
we also sense that it has been Mr. Comley's choice to
go it largely alone.

A representative evangelical strategy for political witness employs what David McKenna has termed the
"Prayer, Preaching, Teaching, and Fellowship" approach. In a roundtable discussion in *Christianity Today*
(April 19, 1985) Dr. McKenna urges the church to pray
for leaders in government; to preach the prophetic message of the gospel and its implications for the individual, the church, the state, and society; to enhance the
teaching ministries of the church to include political
issues; and, when appropriate, to engage in "political
discipleship," where people with political gifts and insights are encouraged to pursue careers as "missionar-
ies without portfolios." By fellowship and the sharing

of resources to meet the needs of church members, McKenna believes the church may model a just society motivated by love. He warns against a confusion of political means with spiritual ends and urges that clergy be careful not to confuse their roles as they relate to political activity.

It strikes us that Steve Comley's story points up the strengths and weaknesses of such a model. Convinced that the Seabrook affair called for justice, and having received some encouragement through prayer and discipleship from his pastor, Mr. Comley has attempted to give substance to his faith convictions. He and his family have paid a heavy price. Doubtless, the Seabrook affair called for this sort of courage; yet the issues involved surely make it quintessentially a *community* matter. Unfortunately, the sort of assistance offered Mr. Comley, valuable and encouraging as it has doubtless been, does not disguise the fact that the issue seems not to have evoked a communal response from the local body of believers. Mr. Comley has been left to develop his "political theology" largely on his own, with the result being a lonely legal battle with only occasional assistance from organizations with overlapping political agendas. Ironically, an issue of fundamental *community* concern has been the subject of a "lone ranger" crusade, in which a single *individual* has taken on the government, and lost. Perhaps there is a better way.

The solitary sojourner model is flawed. If we take our commitment to justice seriously, then we need to involve our churches and communities in the search as well. True, some may be more actively involved than others, but the service cannot be optional. Hence the solitary sojourner model comes up short on the broader question of a comprehensive and lasting witness in politics. As for "Prayer, Preaching, Teaching, and Fellowship," this has a curiously "hands-off" quality in that it sends individuals out to do battle but embraces no ethic of public service. Most disturbing in this respect, it promises little support of the kind Mr. Comley so clearly needed, and risks leaving politics up to a few "political professionals."

Example #3: Keep Sunday Special

What could be more representative of a "Christian" issue than the injunction to "keep holy the Sabbath day"? It is the sort of issue that highlights the contrast between the politics of a privatized Christianity and that of biblically grounded public responsibility. When Protestantism still dominated American culture, blue laws restricting commercial trading and other practices on Sundays were commonplace. In the last thirty years most of these restrictions have been done away with, falling with only moderate resistance to the sway of liberal arguments favoring personal choice and deploring "religious" influences in public policy.

We recall an impressive last-ditch defense by a United Methodist minister in Kentucky as late as 1980, but with the South breached, the end for such laws was in sight. Perhaps this minister was urged on by the highly acclaimed film *Chariots of Fire* (released in the United States about that time), which told the story of Olympic athlete Eric Liddell's refusal to run his one-hundred-meters heat on a Sunday. Ironically, the Eric Liddells of this world seem only to confirm the triumph of an ethic of personal choice. Acts of individual conscience earn respect but also point to the preferred solution: If you don't wish to violate the Sabbath on religious grounds, then don't. Don't shop on Sunday. No one compels you to. Your beliefs are no one else's business, and you can follow them without interfering with the beliefs of those who think differently. All right, you may need to work things out with your employer, but that's up to the two of you and can surely be solved with give and take on both sides. The debate, such as it was, is largely over.

In Britain, it is not over. The Shops Act of 1950, the principal act of Parliament governing Sunday trading, had been targeted for a number of years. During the 1980s, Margaret Thatcher's Conservative government determined to reform it in line with their well-known commitment to freedom of choice. The whole Sunday question seemed ripe for a dose of privatization, and it promised an economic payoff too. So the government, which included several committed Christians—including the Methodist-raised Mrs. Thatcher herself—confidently launched new legislation. And why not? A huge majority in the House of Commons could soak up dissent as it had on every other piece of major legislation, virtually guaranteeing victory.

But the government lost—because a coalition of Christians, trade unionists, industrialists, traditional Anglicans, and traditional Tories rejected the glib formula of individual choice as applied to Sunday trading. The campaign to Keep Sunday Special refused to fight on terms dictated by the other side and developed their own principled basis for the struggle. Their strategy gives us an example of how to develop biblical principles and can be highly instructive for the local congregation.

For a local congregation to accept the status of a privatized belief group with a weak sense of community both theologically and geographically in a culture of rights-based free-market individuals may not constitute an insurmountable barrier to resisting Sunday trading, but it doesn't help either. We suspect it dictates the sort of resistance that would probably be attempted. To begin with, the fourth commandment is unlikely to be read as a norm for human communities *outside* the church. The faithful Lord's Day Observance Society betrays in its title, if not in its teaching, just such an orientation. As long as Sunday is thought of exclusively as the "Lord's Day," it is hard to justify imposing Sabbath practices on those who share no commitment to their Author. And in any case, if the churches treat individual choice as the sole basis of church membership, Christians have no grounds on which to reject an identical formula applied to the matter of Sunday trading.

If, however, the local congregation sees itself as "the people of God in this place," as sojourner-citizens who "live the kingdom" in their public vocations, then the situation is transformed. In the first place, God's sovereignty places limits on individual rights (and the claims to human autonomy that underlie them). Second, the fourth commandment is likely to be seen not in terms of minimal obedience but as an anchor for God's kingdom of justice, peace, and reconciliation. An outward-looking congregation will try to understand biblical principles in their wider application rather than seek only a narrow defense of church interests.

The Keep Sunday Special campaign in Britain is grounded firmly in biblical arguments. Sunday should be kept special because a day of rest is part of God's plan for human beings. A day of rest shows God's love for families by nurturing family life; it protects those of little power and low income and therefore contributes to the restoration of human fellowship. A day of rest releases people from labor and provides an opportunity for contemplating God's goodness. All of these arguments reflect the Old Testament law and testify to the shape of a just and merciful society. Hence most of the objections to unrestricted Sunday trading involve estimates of the effects that violation of these underlying principles may have. This is not the place to go into the legal arguments, the economic effects, or the social implications in any detail. It should be noted, however, that the biblical principles underwriting the Sabbath take direct aim at what Christopher Townsend and Michael Schluter call "an ethos which places too much emphasis on individualism, materialism and economic freedom and too little emphasis on the other facets of human life, in particular the importance of human relationships."[1] It may not come as too much of a surprise to discover that Townsend and Schluter had a particular society in mind: the United States.

As is true of the vast majority of social and political issues, the Sunday trading issue is far from resolved. Fresh legislation, which eventually lifted most restrictions on Sunday trading, was making its way through the British Parliament at the time that this chapter was drafted. But the renewed debate only underscores the weakness of piecemeal politics and the need to develop a permanent, biblically grounded outlook that can engage the ongoing discussion.

As these three very different examples show, there are both biblical and prudential reasons for growing Christian principles for public life in the local congregation. Going it alone has many pitfalls; even going it together will not prevent them unless the congregation also looks to their theology of the church. None of this should be taken to play down the importance of extensive trial and error, for which we know of no adequate substitute.

Conclusion

We are convinced that public responsibility will never become an authentic aspect of the lives of people in churches until they engage in developing those principles out of a sound orientation to the Bible's teachings on kingdom, church, and human beings. If there is a weakness in the extremely useful work done by evangelical thinkers on political questions in recent years, it is that these efforts do not translate their theological and philosophical principles into practical applications for people in churches.[2] The webs of actual relationships, problems, and concerns that pervade the life of the typical Christian family or single person tend to be relatively unreceptive to "outside" ideas or to give them low priority. Yet it has been our contention that the public justice principles we have outlined need no special treatment to be converted into political principles if they are developed in churches. There is no need for a crash course in politics. The authenticity and integrity of the congregation's political principles are best insured by their being developed from a biblically sound view of the church that encourages a "democratic" lay engagement in doing justice.

Of course, within denominations we will find a variety of forms of church government, together with an equally varied range of means for confirming teaching as orthodox. Whatever the situation, however, it is surely the responsibility of lay Christians to insist that Christian teaching include instruction on living out one's vocation in the wider world. This is not a warmed-over 1960s plea to make the gospel "relevant" but rather a call to pastors, bishops, and seminaries to help the people of God recover God's Word for the whole of their lives. Like Jesus' teaching, principles cannot be disconnected from methods. The true test of orthodoxy may lie as much with *where* we teach as in *what* we teach.

STUDY QUESTIONS

1. How persuasive is the authors' argument that piecemeal politics treats politics as an unnatural occupation for Christians? Conversely, are they right to see political involvement as a "natural" activity for Christians?

2. Are there issues in your own congregation that call for biblical rethinking, in the way that the congregation in the chapter rethought the issue of stewardship? How might the theological reorientation of the first three chapters help to accomplish this?

3. The authors caution that "going it alone" is a risky strategy, even if it may be necessary in questions of conscience. How would you respond to a church member in your congregation facing a dilemma similar to the one discussed in the chapter?

4. The authors write of moving out of an "ecclesiastical" frame of reference, of "democratizing" and "broadening the scope" of their discussions. Do the issues you face in your church call for this kind of reorientation?

5. Discuss how two or three major issues—education, the environment, and sexual responsibility, for example—are presently being addressed in your congregation. What changes would you make in the way these are approached?

6. How do you see your congregation's discussion of relevant issues link to and contribute to the discussion of these same issues in your local community?

5

Overcoming
the Language Barrier

I f you've read C. S. Lewis's *That Hideous Strength,* you
probably remember the demented scientists who
lose control of their own speech. One by one they de-
scend into gibberish. As they stumble over their words,
they turn on one another in an orgy of violence. The
passage is one of quite extraordinary power, a judgment
scene drawing on the full range of Lewis's great imagi-
nation. Very few of us would accept that we have suffered the same fate, yet there is more than a passing resemblance to the babbling scientists in our efforts to
give voice to our political principles as Christians.

The problem is not one of failing to speak plain En-
glish but of failing to escape the rhetorical straitjacket
of American public discourse. For here is a language
with a highly selective vocabulary, a language within a
language. Its roots are deep, and like many plants in the

75

natural world, little else can grow in the shade thrown by its leaves and branches.

Aside from the legal and constitutional apparatus of a nation, that nation's identity is perhaps best understood by its culture—the values, outlooks, and assumptions that people share. Culture is a collective property; it is the French, Korean, Sri Lankan, or Finnish way of doing things. So, if I want to convince others within my culture to do such-and-such, I must use the arguments and justifications that work in that culture. For example, President Ronald Reagan called for limits on the size of government, emphasized individual initiative, and insisted on a strong national defense to win voters to the Republican cause in the 1980s. Every one of these policies rested on prominent American cultural values: personal independence, the work ethic, and a tendency to see the world in terms of black and white, good versus evil. Hence, it was not surprising that these went over well with many American voters.

Of course, cultures can usually sustain more than one set of arguments. In the 1960s, Presidents Kennedy and Johnson succeeded in winning support for policies designed to eradicate major social evils, notably poverty— policies that necessitated a considerable degree of government intervention. Indeed, American politicians have been able to recommend opposite strategies in the name of the cultural value attached to a single precept— liberty. Neoconservatives think liberty is best protected the old-fashioned way, by containing government as much as possible and by keeping it off the backs of the people, especially in economic matters. Liberals, on the other hand, have argued for more than a century that the principal threats to liberty at home come not from rogue governments but from the poverty endemic in urban capitalist America. For them, there is no question of stopping with mere equal opportunity; greater equality must be attained through government intervention in the form of a welfare state and related legislation. Diametrically opposed though their policies are, both sides claim to be the true heirs of the American liberal tradition.

In the United States as a whole, the common stock of cultural justifications is a relatively small one. One may express this simply, if a bit misleadingly, by speaking of the narrow range within which American politics moves, a range that excludes communist, most socialist, and all fascist justifications, leaving a narrow band from liberal democratic (Republican and neoconservative) to social democratic (Democratic and liberal) within which the vast majority of this nation's political initiatives fall. Not surprisingly, political scientists have found limited ideological space in which political parties can operate. There is no room, so goes the argument, for more than two parties. Although the left-right image employed here is of questionable accuracy, it is immensely popular and is perpetuated by press and politicians to the point that it has become reality in American politics.

Beyond Liberal and Conservative

The upshot of all this is that policies based on Christian principles find themselves crammed into the existing ideological framework. Take Jesse Jackson, for example. If we accept the popular political options, Jackson's policies seem muddled, to say the least. He sounds like a radical Democrat ("We the people must win!") in his insistence on turning decision making back to those affected by it. He sounds like a Southern conservative in his emphasis on honesty and the integrity of the family. He sounds like a liberal on poverty and civil rights. And he sounds like a conservative on abortion. From the accepted viewpoints of either Democrat or Republican, liberal or conservative, Jackson's views are anomalous or confused.

Upon closer examination, however, we can see that Jesse Jackson quite often takes as his point of departure the biblical narrative, which ties together the diverse strands of his thought. In his understanding, the Bible reveals the truth that we are all beloved children of God who have sinned against him and against one another. Despite our sin, God has provided the means to restore our relationship with him and with one another, and there will be a time of final judgment and justice. On the basis of this narrative, rehearsed and reinforced through his ongoing participation in Black churches as a minister, Jackson is able to articulate a relatively coherent political philosophy and strategy.

Each of us, as a child of God, has value beyond what work or achievements or other human beings may grant. Jackson transforms this into a core precept to be owned by and accorded to every person: self-respect. In one sense it resembles the "natural rights" of individuals claimed by the foremost liberal philosophers, but on examination that resemblance turns out to be a passing one, for the biblical language that secures self-respect is the language of relationship, not of independence or autonomy. And relationships or interdependence are clearly inferred from the idea that we are all God's children, for we are thus related to one another in a familial way. It is this relatedness that undergirds Jackson's conception of "the people," for nothing could be further from a mass democracy of isolated individuals than a conception that treats each of us as a distinct and valued yet related member of the same family.

From this interpretation of Scripture, Jackson crafts a powerful critique of racism and similar divisions in society as illegitimate because they deny our basic relatedness. He calls for reconciliation among nations on the same basis. His rainbow coalition of disparate fringe groups shares this foundation, for Jackson insists that cooperation is not simply desirable but always achievable. The role of statesmen is to appropriate the vision of cooperative life contained in these principles and to reinterpret the elements of American greatness in line with them and away from necessarily divisive images of military and economic might. Thus emerges something quite distinctive in American politics, a vision of public life very much at odds with the respective visions of liberal and social democracy.[1]

Critics of Jackson's political philosophy, including the authors, question a view of Scripture that makes us all God's children without qualification—let alone repentance—or that seemingly puts the sin of one race against another in place of the universal rebellion of all against God (Rom. 3:23). We also question the rather facile way in which Jackson replaces individualism with community as if the ethnic, religious, and racial diversity of the United States could be welded into a seamless whole. These problems alone make the relational scenario sketched here much less appealing. But it strikes us as no coincidence that the uninterrupted fashion in which principles and policies emerge from an understanding of the Bible should be a characteristic of the Black churches in general, and not only of Jesse Jackson's view of Scripture in particular. These churches have traditionally been more community-oriented and politically involved than mainline Protestant churches. We shall shortly argue that evangelicals in the United States may examine fruitfully the traditions expressed in European Christian Democracy, but we would be the first to urge American Christians to look close to home, too. Besides the Black churches (of which Jesse Jackson represents only one segment), the Anabaptists (Amish, Hutterites, and Mennonites) and the Roman Catholic Church also display aspects of what we advocate. In these traditions, too, the debilitating effects of denominationalism have been felt, though less than in the churches of mainline and evangelical Protestantism.

Reclaiming "The Facts of the World"

Due in part to its biblical grounding, Jesse Jackson's political philosophy is realistic in the sense used in this book. If, as we argued in chapter 2, Jesus' teachings on the kingdom of God denounce a counterfeit reality that denies God's sovereignty, then it is a serious matter that Christian thinking about politics should fit the facts, that Christians should set out policies that presuppose God's kingdom at work in the world. Do we legislate for individuals seen solely as consumers of commodities, or for men, women, and children made to image God in this mortal life and in the life everlasting? C. S. Lewis once wrote that he had never met a "mere mortal." Today the foundations of government policy have gone a long way toward stripping down the human person to an individual consumer of things, much as the dynamics of the industrial revolution so often reduced our fathers and grandfathers to mere laborers who tasted little of the fruits of their labor.

The stripping away of the supernatural in assumptions about politics has had profound and lasting consequences. For the political philosopher J. H. Hallowell it led to the dangerous release of coercive power from the protective wall of transcendent authority that had kept it under proper restraint as a legitimate instrument of the offices of government. Once power had been divorced from its true author, the state moved in quickly to claim authorship. And once the state had harnessed itself to political power (in the name of the people who by a social contract equipped it with authority), it would speak of sovereignty in a double sense, not only of the laws of nations respecting control of land and sea but of absolute power without any higher authority to countermand it. In that way the twentieth century's authoritarians and totalitarians were unleashed. Even nationalistic democracies managed to conscript millions of men to take up arms in defense of the state with scarcely a murmur of protest. If a respect for God's authority and justice is to be recovered in the public square, Christians must first recover a sense of public responsibility. And how can they do so unless they also adopt a biblically grounded view of the purposes and limits of government?

How are biblical norms for government and society to be recovered? How may Christians develop a theory of the state? The foundation must be the Scriptures, where we find that government is established by God (Rom. 13:1–7), that governmental authority is thereby derived authority (Rom. 13; Luke 20:20–26), and that human agencies are charged throughout the Old and New Testaments to concern themselves with justice rather than to direct or create their own agendas.

The scriptural foundation is just that, a foundation. Besides the attempt to recover the biblical character of government, Christians must also carefully evaluate the forms that government has taken, the versions of events that they have been told, in order to expose the distortions lying deep within. Christopher Wright, in his book, *An Eye for an Eye: The Place of Old Testament Ethics Today,* remarks that our habitual pattern of ethical

thought is to begin with the individual and work out-
ward, assuming that a certain type of society (or political system) will emerge as a bonus if enough individuals practice the proper ethics. Wright points out that
the Old Testament reverses this order: "Individual ethics
are . . . derivative from the theology of the redeemed
people of God."[2] "Getting back to the Bible" is truly radical in that it would address many areas—theological,
sociological, political—in the process of recovering
God's revelation for us. We must see the world with
God's eyes. J. N. Figgis wrote this perceptively many
years ago:

> What is needed nowadays is that as against the abstract
> and unreal theory of state omnipotence on the one
> hand, and an atomistic and artificial view of individual
> independence on the other, the facts of the world with
> its innumerable bonds of association and the natural-
> ness of social authority should be generally recognized
> and become the basis of our laws, as it is of our life.[3]

In summary, a Christian understanding of politics
must reflect a biblical view of persons, of society, and
of government.

Christian convictions operating through non-Christian structures and institutions make a familiar pattern,
of course. New Testament Christians, for example,
perched uncomfortably on the edge both of Roman authority and Jewish society. It is the usual lot of Christians not to have set the stage but to have the stage set
for them—and to suffer accordingly. Does this mean
that a Christian politics is a rarely attainable luxury?
Far from it. If today Christians are to give an effective
witness to the love of God, if they are to be faithful to
the "facts of the world" in Figgis's words, then they must
not neglect the development of a Christian political vi-

sion. We insert the adjective "Christian" without apology because it describes a radical distinction from the values of secular politics. However constrained such a vision may be by the political circumstances of the age, if it is not developed it will fail even as a peripheral witness. One need hardly remind an evangelical audience that witness is what we are about, or that faithful witness is costly.

Breaching the Barrier

There are several reasons to be optimistic that evangelical Protestants in the United States may be able to develop a better political vocabulary. First, this is already being done by fellow Christians in other traditions, notably by Roman Catholics and by Dutch Protestants, who in the common guise of Christian Democracy have seen their terminology broadly accepted in western European political discourse. For example, the principle of subsidiarity has emerged as part of the discussion over the location of power within the ever-expanding European Union. It has also been undertaken by evangelicals (among others) in the Movement for Christian Democracy (MCD) in Great Britain, whose efforts we will examine later in this chapter, as they may prove particularly instructive for Americans.

British and American evangelicals have much in common, care about similar issues, and have together reached some sort of awareness that their traditions are hampered by problems like privatization and political naivete. In both countries, evangelical Christians have grown disenchanted with the choices offered them by the major political parties; and in both they have struggled with inadequate means of public expression. The pressure-group approach has given Christians some successes, but on both sides of the Atlantic it has done little to educate the Christian public at large.

Britain and the United States have a common political heritage in one especially important sense, for in the modern era both have drawn heavily on the axioms of liberal democracy for policy. At the risk of some oversimplification, we summarize major features of the respective political landscapes as follows: Both countries offer similar sets of choices to voters, as the two major parties in each offer liberal democratic (Conservative/Republican) and social democratic (Labour/Democrat) analyses and policies. Both are, perhaps, reaching the end of an era in which the primary motivation behind policy making has been to limit government interference. Voters in both countries elect *candidates* in single-member districts, instead of the system common in continental Europe whereby political *parties* win seats in the legislature proportionate to their share of the national vote. As a result, both are notorious for the way this machinery suppresses (if not actually stamps out) political initiatives by minor parties.

With the system on their side, the political vocabulary of the major parties has been dominant—and narrow. Important new developments threaten this dominance, however. The first is the end of the cold war. Great Britain and the United States were both ardent prosecutors of the cold war and built up their defense industries accordingly. Both have suffered from the imbalance created in their economies, all the more so as defense is now being downsized. The resulting economic hardship puts new pressure on the old justifications for this policy, and these are weaker than they once were—a possible opening for new ways of defining what is going on.

For Britain, this is already happening for another reason—membership in the European Union. This is having a profound effect on the political vocabulary as politicians wrestle not only with the need to explain, define, and defend Britain's place in Europe but also as Britain encounters the language and style of European politics. It is appropriate, then, to look to Britain, as it faces two sets of pressures for political change, for Christian initiatives that may be of some value to American Christians.

Six Principles for Politics

The political vocabulary developed by the Movement for Christian Democracy is based on six foundational principles: social justice, respect for life, reconciliation, active compassion, wise stewardship, and empowerment.[4] Together, these principles chart a Christian course across the public square. They are not policy statements, but principles from which policy makers take their bearings. They operate in two ways. First, these principles distinguish themselves from their secular counterparts. For example, *justice* in contemporary British (and American) parlance reflects an individualist principle concentrating on the rights of the individual, not of institutions. In contrast, *social justice* recognizes interdependence in all its complex reality; it takes a relational view of people who hold a variety of responsibilities in a diversity of institutions and associations. Second, these principles link issues that are not conventionally associated with each other. The principle of *respect for life,* for example, stresses the interrelation of persons whose lives depend on one another and encompasses such diverse issues as arms sales, abortion, speed limits and road safety, food aid, and sanitation. By stressing the principle rather than the separate issues, emphasis is placed on the sanctity of God's gift of life to each of us.

The principle of *reconciliation* is familiar to Christians in its vertical dimension, where it is exemplified in the teaching, death, and resurrection of Jesus Christ. The horizontal dimension brings us face to face with the countless ways in which humans have substituted self-ishness or hostility or have permitted long-standing disputes to foster hatred across generations and between peoples. To articulate a commitment to reconciliation means to concentrate on developing new and better justifications for relevant policies and institutions without ignoring the importance of personal motives and actions. Will a given policy allow another nation to retain self-respect during a dispute, or does it humiliate the other? Are demands for racial or gender equality accompanied by reasonable means of achieving their fulfillment? What are the mechanisms whereby repentance and forgiveness may be publicly declared and unity will be restored? The last instance embraces everyone from the criminal who has paid his debt to society to the bankrupt given protection from her creditors; in both cases, it seems, unfinished business remains. The criminal still needs to be reconciled to society and to his victim(s) and the debtor to her creditors.

By *active compassion*, the Movement for Christian Democracy means the intentional caring that Jesus practiced and its implementation in the services offered to, and the relationships established with, those who suffer or are at a disadvantage. For many Christians, the lack of active compassion that is evident in welfare systems is their reason for rejecting public welfare programs in favor of voluntary initiatives. Such a response cannot be squared with the idea of doing politics Christianly. Not only is it a defeatist response that supposes governments cannot be so crafted to encourage justice, but it is also an abdication of responsibility all the more evident when the issue is broadened to include the quality of the relationships between rich and poor nations. The idea of *wise stewardship* is a powerful means of cutting across common notions of ownership and control of land or other resources that have tended to dominate Western thought. It is high time stewardship was released from its nearly exclusive association with managing church budgets! The biblical idea of stewardship transforms our relationship to these resources with far-reaching effects on policies for their use and conservation. It is worth speculating how a simple change in language from "private ownership" to "private stewardship" could, in the long run, affect housing prices, the behavior of landlords, or the market for cars or luxury goods, let alone questions about the direction of environmental policy. The MCD does not, of course, claim that this is a unique idea. After all, many farming families have practiced excellent stewardship in caring for, living from, and raising a family on the farm and then passing it on for the next generation to use. Sadly, it has become increasingly difficult for many families to continue to practice such stewardship in the face of mounting costs, and this strong model will soon be largely lost.

Empowerment has often been on the lips of revolutionaries, going to the heart of the solutions they seek. And indeed, of all the principles, we believe this is the one that needs the most careful handling and perhaps some rethinking by the MCD. In general, it is a call for an end to unhealthy relations of power in which the lives of people, and sometimes whole nations, are hemmed in by the misuse of power either through specific acts or by institutional structures, or in relationships intended for other purposes. Empowerment is, we feel, insufficiently qualified by the MCD to serve as a general remedial principle. They seem to mean simply "respect for the right of people to live their lives openly before God."[5] God is the author of power—it originates in him alone and is made perfect in weakness, not in the pursuit of self-interest. The MCD has not disentangled the legitimate (and artificial) function of a right to self-determination from the illegitimate claims to natural rights and human autonomy.

Here, then, are six axioms for doing politics Christianly. In seeking to distinguish a Christian political vocabulary that can integrate fragmented discourse, the MCD may help us to change the way we speak and think about politics and the way we go about trying to make public policy. These six principles represent a starting point for a vocabulary to bring God's truth to public life in a conscious challenge to the popular vocabulary of politics. Perhaps the best way to respond to the principles is to discuss them at length in a study group, and we recommend this below. We must stress their partial nature, however. On their own, sets of principles may turn out to be wooden and lifeless. They are best understood as contributing to the process of developing a biblical view of all of life, of thinking as citizens and sojourners, of living the reality of the kingdom, and of looking to life among the people of God as a natural source for ideas and policies. To use another biblical figure, Paul calls on Christians to have "the mind of Christ" (Phil. 2:5; 1 Cor. 2:16). We need to employ a number of means to honor Paul's exhortation. To do politics faithfully in a setting pervaded by an unbiblical terminology requires that we get a clear grasp of Christian principles and develop equally clear means of giving expression to them.

Without a much lengthier discussion we cannot fully assess the application of these principles in the American setting, but we are optimistic about their applicability. First, as we observed earlier, the similarities between British and American evangelical Christianity and the current British and American political climates suggest that these principles may prove useful in both places. Second, both British and American Christians frequently express a desire to transcend partisan rhetoric but have taken little action because they have lacked an alternative language and organization. The six principles come at an opportune time to foster just the sort of debate that Christians seem to want to have. There remain two final issues: meeting the objections of those who find our discussion here esoteric, fruitless, or perfectionist and contrasting our prescriptions for a Christian political vocabulary with the activist prescriptions commonly found in American public discourse both inside and outside the churches.

Defending a Christian Vocabulary

We anticipate a number of realist objections to this part of our project. Realists might argue that our account of the difficulties involved in crafting a new vocabulary underscores the fruitlessness of the attempt. They might argue that our search is really for perfect rather than contingent categories, which are all that a fallen world offers. They might complain that we are wasting our resources on a fruitless undertaking instead of training Christians to know and use the existing language of politics. If, as we have asserted, the problem is partly the amateur status of Christians in politics, then professionalism is better served by training Christians to think politically, not by giving them a vocabulary that few outside the faith will comprehend.

These are important objections. Responding to them permits us to reflect on the nature of politics. Contesting existing terminology is not a peripheral exercise. Rather, it lies at the heart of politics, because this terminology is what constitutes the political world. Political philosophy engages in this exercise constantly. It is not something new, nor is the possibility of rejection unique to Christians. With little effect in his own lifetime, Karl Marx sought to introduce and spread the belief that all history is the history of class struggle, an idea that came up against the same individualistic frame of reference that we have discussed in these pages. Although its success was not, thankfully, universal, the Marxist achievement was to reinvigorate the collectivist idea from where liberalism had left it to languish. Several centuries earlier, Christian thinkers, such as Augustine, had upset all the seemingly settled categories of the classical political world, relocating vital concepts like justice, introducing new and uncomfortable contrasts between Christian community and earthly societies. True justice, Augustine challenged Cicero, is not of this world. The Roman world, the Western tradition, was never the same again.

The development of a political vocabulary has solid precedent in the Reformed and Roman Catholic traditions, which have an impressive record of political engagement. The Dutch theologian and statesman Abraham Kuyper understood very well the wisdom of combining an "antithetical" approach (developing Christian principles in the face of conflicting secular perspectives) with an attempt to engage the wider world. In the long run, you cannot engage the wider world Christianly unless you have first distinguished a set of principles with which to engage it. Therefore,

Christians cannot use the common, secular under-standing of reality without placing their project at risk. Are we dealing with kingdom reality or simply with what passes for reality in a cynical culture that has lost or denied any hint of the transcendent? What we have termed here "a set of principles" is often rendered as a Christian "worldview" or "world-and-life view" but amounts to a disciplined obedience to what God has revealed in the Scriptures. In Roman Catholic thought, the principle that individual enterprise be subsumed to the common good has, since the rise of capitalism, been of incalculable importance to Christian and non-Christian alike. To some extent this thinking is re-sponsible for social-market approaches in Europe, where the Roman Catholic tradition is strong; in Britain and America, where that tradition has been peripheral, free-market thinking has tended to prevail instead.

To summarize, we cannot accede to the realist ob-jections outlined above without accepting too much of the status quo; liberal or conservative does not ade-quately describe secular politics, let alone Christian op-tions. Nor can we do so without abandoning our cri-tique of the churches. If we are convinced that there are serious shortcomings in the way the churches proclaim and practice a theology of the kingdom, then we must seek to correct these shortcomings as constructively as possible.

We have reached this stage of the argument by sev-eral steps. First, we described and discussed the prob-lem of the amateur evangelical eager to engage public life but often ill-equipped for it. To address this dilemma, we urged attention to Scripture's perspectives on God's people (sojourner-citizens), the kingdom, and the church. We urged Christians to study these per-spectives in their congregations and to derive from them principles for life both in the churches and in the

wider world. We would stress again the need to begin
and continue this project within the local congregation, not to go it alone. We urge Christians to take time,
to exercise charity in every aspect of the project's development, and to reckon with the sheer difficulty of
the undertaking. Our aim is not to mire the local congregation in contemplation of abstract theological questions, but to begin the task of addressing Christian public responsibilities in the light of the full scope of the
gospel. Ours, then, is a thoroughly practical undertaking whose goal is faithful obedience to God, an obedience reflected in the faithfulness of our biblical vision,
the implementation of that vision, and the communal
basis from which it is launched.

STUDY QUESTIONS

1. In general, how difficult do you find communi-
   cating the dynamics of your church's conception
   of the human condition to those outside the
   church? For example, how would you discuss the
   biblical theology of the church with your non-
   Christian neighbor?
2. As you reconsider issues like stewardship, care for
   the environment, abortion, and world peace in
   the light of the context of the discussion in this
   chapter, how adequate do you find the conventional vocabulary for talking about these issues?
3. Can you think of other issues (perhaps ones that
   you have already discussed in your congregation)
   that call for reexpressing in more appropriate
   terms?
4. Discuss the authors' claim that in view of its in-

adequacies, Christians need to reformulate the language of politics. Is this necessary? Is it realistic?

5. How effective are the six principles of the Movement for Christian Democracy described in the text? What could be done in the American context to help Christians develop principles like these?

6. What steps should your church or study group take next?

6

Christian Principles for Politics

The United States is a liberal democratic nation that needs its Christian communities to overhaul its view of liberty, to transform its view of people, and to challenge its view of nation. In this closing chapter we move the discussion to the level of political systems. We examine the basic characteristics of liberal democracy as it has developed in the United States, discuss the deficiencies of liberal democracy from a scriptural point of view, and present a Christian Democratic alternative for America's future.

America's Liberal Democracy

The American form of government, liberal democracy, is a design for a free society, a society that has

largely dispensed with traditional ways because these
were never firmly rooted in American soil. Instead, the
United States developed at an early stage a vigorous
commitment to a society that would maximize individual liberty. Several forces came together to create this
commitment. The late eighteenth century represented
the apex of Enlightenment ideas about natural rights
and the human creativity and growth they promised.
The older theological orientation of America's Puritans
dovetailed neatly, if rather surprisingly, with these ideas.
The Puritans would not have looked favorably on either the claims of human autonomy or the pervasive
air of confidence breathed by the Enlightenment. Nev-
ertheless, in Puritan pessimism with respect to power
and sin, and in Puritan activism, which urged men to
take up their vocations as industriously as possible and
held up the faithful community as a chosen "city on a
hill," lay solid foundations for a government of limited
scope and a society of furious individual activity, vision,
and purpose.

A third influence, more mundane but no less transforming, was land. The vast virgin spaces were deemed
empty by the colonists, as empty they certainly were of
feudal trappings, if not of natives. Land turned the most
prosaic of writers rhapsodic. Land lent to the liberal
ideas of the Enlightenment the means of practical fulfillment. One really could imagine, with Hector St. John
de Crevecoeur or Thomas Jefferson or a host of like-
minded writers, a republic of yeoman farmers in which
the sheer amount of land available, coupled with the
physical limits on each person's ability to cultivate it,
not only encouraged liberty but also promised equality. Above all, liberal democracy could be rendered ut-
terly ordinary, not the stuff of endless European debates,
not an abstract political theory, but a plain and simple

description of the way America would naturally govern itself.

The political disputes that spawned the Revolution simply confirmed, to most Americans, the stark differences between old and new, between government by remote, coercive authority and self-government. The gulf between the two was made wider by the conviction that originated with the Puritans that the virtue of the latter confirmed the vice of the former, and many a pulpit rang with colorful denunciations of the British "antichrist." It was surely no surprise either that Jefferson should exaggerate and elevate the catalog of complaints against King George (which occupy most of the text of the Declaration of Independence) to a litany of moral crimes against the "inalienable" rights of the people.

So liberal democracy got off to a strong start in the United States because its foundations had been shaping the mindset of Americans for a century or more and their coming together at the Revolution made them naturally and mutually reinforcing.

Unlike several European countries in which Christianity (as manifested by the Roman Catholic Church in particular) looked suspiciously on democracy for much of the nineteenth century and embraced it wholeheartedly only after World War II, the United States saw an early linkage between the two. The Revolutionary War generation urged democratic procedures as the only fitting procedures for a free people who had thrown off a foreign monarchy. Although the leaders of the Revolution—the "gentlemen," as historians refer to them—spoke of their new form of government as a republic, ordinary Americans acted as if the design was intentionally and principally democratic.[1] At the forefront of these ordinary Americans were evangelicals who dis-

trusted government hierarchies as much as they did ecclesiastical ones. Beginning with their own battles to
resist the extension of authority by eastern seminaries
to the western frontier, they forged an ethos for America that has become widely accepted. The American attitude toward politics has been described as an antipolitical political culture. Americans distrust remote
decision makers and prefer private initiatives to public,
governmental ones.

Democratization won impressive victories. Those radical democratic reformers, the Populists, failed to elect
a president in 1896 and later, but the reforms they
championed were almost all adopted into law. Before
the new century was very old, candidate selection had
been wrested from party bosses and placed in the hands
of party voters. Initiative, referendum, and recall al-
lowed voters to propose and pass legislation in tandem
with, or even in defiance of, the legislature, and to turn
elected officials out of office; U.S. senators were elected
by popular vote and not by state legislatures. Regulation of freight charges on railroads, regulation of utili-
ties, and federal income tax were all reality.

In the later twentieth century, democratization pro-
ceeded apace. Ordinary Americans began to desert the
political parties in large numbers in the 1960s, a phenomenon linked to rising levels of education and the
coming of television as well as to the party reforms of
the early years of the century. The 1970s and 1980s saw
the rise of independent registrations to unprecedented
heights. Many citizens now found their most mean-
ingful political participation in the web of interest
groups that spread rapidly in the same period. Formally,
only a few new initiatives were taken, such as lowering
the voting age by constitutional amendment in 1971.
There were and continue to be calls for direct election
of the president. There are enthusiastic calls for direct

voting via TV hookups. Opinion poll results have become staples of the evening news.

If these reforms all bear the stamp of the people,
democracy's victory has been a hollow one. The earlier
electoral reforms in particular so weakened the parties
that voters lost the services of their single most effective advocate, the kind of institution necessary to their
political education and the only institution that could
really connect them to government. The substitutes
have been poor. By the 1970s it was evident that an ill-
informed, apolitical (that is, privatized) electorate was
simply no match for the techniques of modern campaigning. Increasingly volatile in its choices, the electorate can no longer make itself heard distinctly as a
plural entity, due largely to the banal forms of com-
munication that dominate modern campaigns: campaign commercials, weak coverage of candidates' and
parties' principles and policies, spasmodic reporting of
news by a medium overshadowed by its need to enter-
tain. And, of course, television has ripped apart the already loose patchwork of communities into so many
single strands. We watch politics alone from our living
rooms, not together.

For those who have turned to interest groups to give
their ideas voice and influence, there have been more
illusions to shatter. Few interest groups, even so-called
citizens' groups, are directed by their members' preferences, and the most powerful groups still represent
those old "interests"—finance, commerce, big business.
Interest groups also remain stubbornly middle class, for
it is this sector of the population that can bring the resources of organization, time, money, and experience
to the formation and maintenance of groups.

In appearance, democracy is everywhere in America.
In reality, the political system is patchily democratic,
the bureaucracy unresponsive, and policy making the

preserve of the few rather than the many. Where once antipolitical feeling kept government within prescribed limits, now its descendent, a privatized indifference, gives appointed and elected officials considerable freedom of action.

Federalism and Nationalism

We gain a fresh perspective on liberal democracy if we now turn from the people to their nation. The Constitution's framers seized the term "federal" to describe their new form of government, leaving their opponents tagged with the unflattering label "antifederalists." It has been customary for students of federalism to devote considerable space in their books to this, their largest example. The trouble is, the United States has never been as intentionally (or happily) federalist as the name implies.

At its inception, the United States possessed many pluralist features: thirteen independent states with well-developed, distinctive political traditions; multifarious subcultures both racial and religious; a strong tradition of local decision making (especially in New England); a tendency to equate political liberty with individual rights and with decision making at the lowest possible level. It would not have been unreasonable to expect the new republic to enshrine and protect these pluralistic characteristics in a truly federal system—one of shared powers. For a few brief years, this was the case. Under the Articles of Confederation, little power flowed out of the states to the central government.

The Philadelphia Convention changed all that, however. The framers got the nation to accept a system based on a much more powerful national government. States retained powers on paper, but their best means of checking the new federal government was not by recourse to paper checks but through the representatives they sent to the new Congress.[2] The much-condemned pork barrel may be the earlier federalism's last stand, for ever since raising revenue became a chiefly federal government power, states and localities have striven to divert some of the flow of programs and funds in their direction.

States' rights were on the defensive from the time the Constitution was ratified, and they have remained there. In nearly every major confrontation between state and federal governments, the courts have sided with the federal government. It did not help that "states' rights" became a code word for the defense of slavery or that slavery's battles had to be fought all over again a century later during the civil rights movement.

If political federalism turned out to be hollow, what of the pluralist society with its increasingly colorful ethnic and religious aspect? By the late nineteenth century, American society became genuinely multicultural, albeit WASP elements were dominant. Society's pluralism was denied adequate political expression, however. Instead, political leaders stressed national themes. Rather than imagining a differentiated society, the United States was to be a "melting pot." Its liberties were to be extended to the new immigrants, who were to be rendered Americans as quickly as possible. Let us have no more hyphenated Americans, declared Theodore Roosevelt. Woodrow Wilson took Roosevelt's metaphor one step further, describing the hyphen as "a dagger aimed at the republic's heart." The United States was to be one nation, one community.

For many Christians at the turn of the century, such a unitary, national vision illuminated the role that

Christianity should play. For Walter Rauschenbusch and the social gospel movement in the early part of this century, Christian foundations and culture made the nation Christian; conversely, to be Christian was to take the national way. Thus Christianity collapsed easily into nationalism and the church into the nation. The social gospel movement is now long past, but its legacy remains in the difficulty Christians have in finding any other than a nationalist vision for American society to go hand in hand with an individualist vision for American citizens. And since nationalist is meant as undifferentiated, it treats society as a potentially unitary community. Such a vision flirts with nondemocratic government and risks erasing the church-state distinction to the detriment of the liberal freedoms, principal among which is religious liberty.

The Christian nationalist vision has been little realized in the twentieth century. The story of religious liberty we visited in chapter 3 has followed a different course. We saw there how liberal individualism recognized for religion only an *individual* right of conscience, and how the concept of a "wall of separation" between church and state confined religious expression to the private sphere of life, with debilitating effects on the orientation and mission of Protestant churches—how ironic in a Protestant culture!

It remains simply to stress the connection between this treatment of religious liberty and the parallel development of a political ethos centered not on persons, groups, shared powers, pluralism, and the state, but on the individual and the state alone. The United States developed as a liberal democracy, not as a pluralist or consociational one. Liberal democratic values encouraged free-market capitalism based on individual competition rather than social-market capitalism more respectful of group and community interests. Americans easily resisted the collectivist values of socialism and communism along with authoritarianism and totalitarianism, *but they excluded the genuine federalism that was also part of the American heritage.* They stood for an individual liberty that was universal in scope but also narrow in its viewpoint. Certainly those whose imaginations were steeped in the Scriptures, as so many American imaginations were, should have been able to do better.

Christian Response to Liberal Democracy

This brief historical sketch suggests that American democracy differs importantly from democracy in societies whose political institutions and instincts have been superimposed on traditional societies. Those societies, too, feel the pressures associated with television, with the rise of individualism, and so forth, but they have often found it possible to feed their democratic impulses through structures and communities that keep people more connected to one another. As proof of this, compare any European political party with any American one. The former are ideologically and organizationally integrated, the latter loosely structured on both counts. Or, more vividly, compare European towns with American ones. Community in the sense of simple human transactions still exists to an impressive extent in Europe, where very large numbers of people still walk or bike to work, school, shops, church, or recreation. In the United States, on the other hand, the car, once a symbol of freedom, has become a necessity, for without it, the suburb is a prison devoid of the basics of human life. American democracy floats free of communal tethers to a great extent; it is no coincidence that it has developed most distinctly the features of *liberal* democracy. Anchored by few ties of tradition or local community, the central values of American democracy are those of the free, independent, self-governing individual. Sustaining those values may once have been merely a difficult task; it is now an astonishingly expensive one, requiring huge economic resources, to say nothing of the professional apparatus needed to treat the emotional and physical side effects of the lifestyle to which those values have given rise. Consider, for example, the funds spent on interstate highways and city expressways for the private car, or the increased market for psychiatric and counseling services.

The usual response from Christians to this sort of analysis is to call for developing character and all the attendant desiderata of a free people. They say that without an informed, intelligent, and morally upright citizenry, democracy is clearly in peril, especially liberal democracies, which rely more heavily on individual participation than do other forms. We agree—cautiously. For the usual prescriptions are offered within precisely that individualistic frame of reference and are incapable of asking whether it is the right frame of reference. Must individuals always come first, and society be their by-product? What, precisely, is the proper relationship between society and individual rights in a fallen world? Can individualism survive character development, or is character development along biblical lines fundamentally incompatible with it?

This is where the churches come in, because they fulfill something missing in many other educational institutions. They are, after a fashion, communities and embrace values that are other-directed. Their Bible (not least the Lord's Prayer) is best understood as directed to a community—and is best studied together[3]—though doing so is hardly in fashion! They prize individual liberty, but at the heart of the gospel lies a rejection of human autonomy, let alone self-gratification, as the way to salvation. Their God is omnipotent but draws human beings into relationship with himself not by force but by love. His Son, with all this power at his command, set the supreme example of self-sacrifice and manifested that power in weakness, not brute strength. Here lies the true material from which to build character in democracies. Many of our churches, however, are ersatz communities at best, struggling against the "belief group" legacy bequeathed to them by liberal individualism itself. In sheer physical terms, let us remind ourselves that many churches are also victims of the postwar suburban scattering. They can assemble "communities" once, perhaps twice, a week—communities of people who simply do not see each other the rest of the time.

To state the case soberly, the sources of a democracy more in keeping with America's plural society certainly exist in the United States (we could go beyond churches to civic groups or unions to make the point more clearly), but the sources themselves have been shaped decisively by the larger culture whose values are those of liberal democracy. And as we noted in chapter 3, the Constitution itself disposes of the multifaceted character of the body of Christ by dissolving it in the acid of personal preference and rights of conscience. Renewing the sources of pluralist democracy is essential to any lasting influence that Christianity may have on the political system.[4]

Both the church, considered in earlier chapters, and the political system, discussed in this one, contain democratic elements. Both suffer if democracy is force-fitted into an individualistic-nationalistic frame of reference. For churches, this can entail wholesale distortion of the New Testament view of the body of Christ, its mission in the world, and the ends of salvation. For the political order, it entails a weakened democracy with a volatile and vulnerable electorate, democratic in appearance only.

From our earlier discussions, it is clear that the state of the churches and the state of the political order are indeed connected. Christian preferences joined political ones to secure the denomination as the distinctive form of religion in America and to establish the individualistic solution to the question of religious liberty as a right of conscience. Evangelical instincts underwrote America's activist and antipolitical political culture. Addressing these crises in church and state calls for a common project, not two separate ones. To live as the church, Christ's body, and God's people, Christians must recover a real, biblical view of who we are. We could ground this view in Jesus' summary of the law: The law commands us to put God first in our personal and corporate life as the sovereign Lord of creation, our Father; and it commands us to build relationships with one another that balance freedom with responsibility, individual wants with corporate needs, the requirements and proper authority of church administration and teaching with service to the people of God in their daily life and work. These commitments and corrections also underwrite a healthy democracy. Fundamentally, to grant God's sovereignty is to deny individual autonomy and to refuse to legitimize that false foundation for personal rights. For we are not, in fact, autonomous individuals whose fulfillment lies in enlarging the consumer ethic of our time; we are creatures made in the image of the Creator-God to know and love him, creatures set to love and care for the created order, creatures of place and multiple associations—family, tribe, nation—whose fulfillment lies in voluntary obedience to God and service to one another, and in a freedom to pursue both.

The urgency with which Christians ought to consider the vital resource they already have cannot be underestimated. For they possess democracy's most important preconditions:

- A faith directing them to obedience to one higher than themselves, in whose service and in whose service alone their lives find fulfillment
- A training in the collective good
- A tradition of service to others, especially the powerless
- A commitment to freedom

This brings us full circle to the sojourner-citizen. If that phrase captures the irony we hoped to convey in its hyphenation (sojourners make the best citizens), it falls a bit short, too. For sojourners make the best citizens when they enter the public sphere *as members of their faith communities,* not artificially separating the former from the latter but bringing values, principles, language, plans, and policies developed as members of the body of Christ into that permissive arena we call liberal democracy.

Christian Democracy

Christians have subjected liberal democracy to this sort of criticism ever since its emergence in the nineteenth century. During the past century, however, these have been European and Catholic Christians more often than Anglo-American, Protestant ones. One of the tragedies of American politics has been its impoverished language, as we observed in chapter 5. It is quite possible that some of our readers will have concluded, on the strength of our criticisms of liberal democracy, that we want the alternative—an invasive government, state socialism, and collectivism. When political rhetoric offers only more government as an alternative to less government, such a conclusion is understandable. But it is false. In truth, the Christian conception of government and society on which we base our call to build a democracy that looks to communities as much as to individuals is not collectivism, nor is it a halfway house. It is not a temporary shelter cobbled together from irreconcilable beliefs by spiritual sleight of hand. It is not the impossible meeting place of left and right.

Dispensing with left or right, more or less rhetoric, we see the Christian perspective as an unexplored third corner of a triangle that Americans have always viewed as a simple straight line from left wing to right wing. But it's not a new vision by any means, as we made plain in discussion of the Movement for Christian Democracy's six principles. Christian Democracy has an impressive pedigree stretching back a hundred years in forms both Catholic and Protestant, and in important senses drawing on a much older, predemocratic Christian tradition.[5] In its view of state and society, it counters liberal democracy decisively at every turn with transformative rather than destructive criticisms: Where liberal democracy is *individualist,* Christian Democracy is *personalist;* and from this doctrine of personality it follows that Christian Democracy is also *relational* rather than *competitive,* and concerned for the *plural structures and authorities* of society rather than for exclusive grants of power to the *individual* and the *state.*

Writing of the rise of European Christian Democracy after World War II, Michael Fogarty summarized its distinctive political contribution as follows:

At the centre was the idea that the purpose of social and
political action is to enable the development of personality in the light of the value attributed to it in revelation: partly through ensuring the necessary material
conditions, but above all by enabling people to develop
the capacity to make the most of their lives in every
sphere from religion to work and leisure: not simply as
individuals, but in and through solidarity with communities of all kinds from the family and local community to the nation and the world, bringing in professional, class, and inter-class solidarity on the way.[6]

It is easy to forget that the beginnings of modern liberal democracy, with its great emphasis on the rights of
the individual, were more critical and corrective in tone
and purpose than they were constructive. Great writers
like Locke and Jefferson turned to the language of natural rights because these provided exceptionally powerful justification for rebellion, together with com-
pelling arguments against the exercise of governmental
power without the consent of the people. Individual
rights, then, were and are primarily defensive weapons
protecting people from arbitrary exercise of power
against their will. Locke certainly imagined the use of
these weapons as the central mechanism by which just
government (government by consent under the rule of
law) would be regularized. But in fashioning these powerful weapons for politics, he displaced every other traditional component of society. Locke's peculiar "society" contains only adults: there are no families, no
children, no guilds—in short, none of the groupings
that make up actual societies. In Locke's society, individuals communicate with each other more like nations
than persons. Every relationship is a contract secured
by individual choice, leaving no room for bonds of fam-

ily love and affection, or for associations founded on religious belief and tradition, or for community solidarity born of common circumstances and culture. In fact, Locke's liberal society is not much of a society at all but a political arena where strangers follow laws of contract to soften the clash of selfish interests.[7] Or, as Margaret Thatcher once declared, "There is no such thing as society, only individuals."

Now, of course, exclusively self-interested individuals resemble people no more than Locke's contractual state resembles a flesh-and-blood society. Such individuals define themselves in *competition* with others whose needs and wants always threaten them; real people define themselves in *concert* with others to whom they look for mutual help, love, sustenance, and so forth. In the body of Christ, we are individual members of one another; our individuality makes the body whole. Hence our freedom is less usefully a freedom to do whatever we wish (John Winthrop and like-minded Puritans acknowledged the presence of such freedom but termed it *license*, not *liberty*) but more a contribution of our unique selves to God's service. The phrase "whose service is perfect freedom" captures a reassuring scriptural paradox: Just as the power of God is perfected in the demonstrated weakness of Jesus on the cross, so our own beloved identity—as Joan or Marco or Siobhan or Roger—is enhanced by its surrender, not by the assertion of our wills.

A Christian personalism is not a rejection of individuality but of individualism. When Jesus summarized the law, he compared the love we should have for others with the love we have already for ourselves. It is a doctrine of personality that connects individuality with community. It actively rejects individualism, seeing it as a counterfeit of Christian doctrine, a counterfeit that is for that reason just as mistaken when operating at the heart of politics. Political action based on individual will must carry the resulting distortion of personality all the way from principle to policy. Individualism in economic matters can hide the assumption that all people have the means to make real choices. Individualism risks turning a blind eye to age, resources, and experience in fields from personal health to criminal justice. Individualism threatens to redefine natural communities like family and church as mere voluntary associations. For the family, the mutual responsibilities of marriage are put at risk to the detriment of children especially; for the church, there is the debilitating slide into belief-group status, which we discussed in previous chapters.

Christian Democracy is hostile to individualism, on biblical grounds, but it does not reject personal freedoms and legal protections. Rather, it recognizes that in their proper context they have been and remain enormously successful in defying tyrannical regimes and transforming traditional ones. Unlike those who view the First Amendment as a sort of alternative constitution, however, Christian Democracy is not content to erect the entire structure of government and society on the liberal freedoms alone but seeks to safeguard vital communal forms of human liberty as well as individual freedom. Hence it must reject liberal democracy's reduction of society to the individual and the state and the reduction of law to individual rights and state sovereignty. If society is altogether richer, more diversified, and more pluralistic than liberal democracy allows, the political order should reflect that richness, diversity, and pluralism. Individual liberties expressed as rights have their place, but in Christian Democracy that place is to protect people from political oppression, not to weaken the protection that schools, families, businesses, and other forms of association, both voluntary and natural, must also enjoy.

The Christian Democratic view of government is anchored by a small number of principles that complement the doctrine of personalism outlined above. Chief among these is *subsidiarity,* which urges that authority be granted to make decisions as close as possible to those affected by them where that is practicable but which also insists that the state (or higher authority) must act itself where necessary. This is Christian Democracy's way of bringing both freedom and protection to the many traditional, familial, and professional communities that make up a society. For example, business decisions ought to be taken inside a business with as little outside interference as possible, but the state retains responsibility and authority to act in matters such as the health and personal safety of employees. There is no reason why the company should not devise appropriate health and safety rules, of course, since its personnel are best equipped to understand the processes and characteristics of production, but deference to this knowledge and experience should not be an excuse for government to draw back on its ultimate responsibility to do justice.

Closely related is the principle that authority should be an *enabling authority.* Though subsidiarity limits government intervention, legitimate government intervention must be vigorous and up to the task that belongs to it. And yet it must also be turned toward those it serves. There is no place for the exercise of power out of proportion to that necessary to serve (in this case) the health and safety of employees and the public.

Further, if health and safety rules are to be largely designed within the company, they should be crafted by all the members of that company (or their representatives). The principle of *solidarity* recognizes the presence of competing interests among the groups involved in any enterprise but urges them to see that cooperation is in the long-term interest of those groups. These words were first drafted during the storm of protest that greeted the British government on the announcement that thirty-one coal mines were to be closed and thirty thousand miners were to lose their jobs in the fall of 1992. Although it paid lip service to subsidiarity in its support for closer European union, the government violated both the principle of subsidiarity (for there was no local consultation) and the related principle of *change with continuity* in the case of the miners. The latter accepts change—industrial development, for example—but insists that it be accompanied by protection for those on whom the changes have an impact. In the United States, countless communities have suffered the effects of hostile takeovers in violation of these principles: The local management is dismissed or demoted, and their knowledge of the company's place in the community is lost. Remote decision makers decide the fate of company and community. The principle of subsidiarity would certainly not absolve local community leaders from anticipating change and planning to meet it, but such planning takes time and is best done with the full participation of all concerned, including local managers of the company whose future may precipitate the coming changes.

Christian Democracy underscores these principles by emphasizing that justice in the economy be commutative (in other words, that dealing be fair), social (placed in an identifiable framework of management and distribution), and distributive (meeting the needs that the marketplace alone does not provide).

In Christian Democracy we begin to see the distinctive shape of an authentic Christian politics. As Professor Fogarty observes, the entire package of Christian Democratic principles takes us well beyond the idea that

Christian politics means defending church interests.
Here is an ideology able to compete with liberal democracy and to offer a comprehensive challenge to its vision for state, society, and individual. Here, to return to
our nautical metaphor, is one vessel equipped for the
sea lanes of public life, not for the stagnant backwaters
of privatized religion.

Christian Democracy in America

We write, to this point, as though the Christian politics we would embrace must be imported from Europe,
of all places. Didn't Americans flee Europe to flee religious persecution? Why would a perspective developed
for societies very different from the United States be seriously worth importing for application here? Would it
play in Peoria?

In the 1980s, business magazines began to take serious note of a new phenomenon in the automobile industry: the assembly of cars from components built all
over the world. The Ford Escort was dubbed the "world"
car. The analogy to Christian Democracy is not perfect,
but it works. Christian Democracy emerged as a coherent Christian understanding for politics not out of exclusively European components built in Rome and as-
sembled in Brussels, so to speak. Far from it. Long before
the *Partito Popolare Italiano* organized in the early 1920s,
long before Abraham Kuyper and Pope Leo XIII wrestled with the rise of liberalism and industrialism and its
implications for society in 1891, Americans struggled
against a combination of imperialism and religious in-
tolerance in a classic confrontation from which they
emerged with sharply developed notions of personal
rights and limited government. Nor was the American

struggle itself original, for it grew out of the earlier British struggle to limit the power of the king, a struggle no less vitally connected to religious freedom, and one that gave rise to parliamentary democracy. To put the case for the United States even more strongly, Americans "solved" the problem of Constantine—of Christianity's long association with empire—well over a century before most Europeans recognized the problem, let alone applied themselves to it. In its Roman Catholic manifestation, Christian Democracy is a late marriage between Christianity and democratic principles. The core Christian Democratic principles outlined in this chapter derive from *issues* tackled comprehensively by colonial America—although the Americans proffered *solutions* that bear little resemblance to contemporary Christian Democracy.

There, of course, is the rub. Christian Democracy was, for America, the road *not* taken. The American attempt to combine the removal of religious factionalism from public life with the free exercise of religion exacted a high price from genuine religious freedom. Americans "solved" the problem of tyrannical government with limited government. Even after the industrial revolution, when they found themselves with big government anyway, Americans remained loyal to their suspicion of governmental authority.

Study of religion in America in the eighteenth century continues to contribute precious insight into Christian politics, as does examination of European politics of the late nineteenth century and especially of the half century since World War II. Europeans came to their belated confrontation with empire with some advantages that the Americans lacked: They observed the rise of nationalism in the liberal state, and they faced totalitarianism and world war in ways that gave their understanding an international dimension. Thus, they recovered a centuries-old tradition of thinking about people and society and power in societies that had not become as aggressively individualistic as the United States. Now a new opportunity for shaping political thought is upon us, as the collapse of communist totalitarianism gives Eastern Europeans, Ukrainians, and Russians their own opportunities to craft a distinctively Christian politics after imperialism. Roman Catholic and Lutheran insight from Poland and East Germany promises to refresh Christian Democracy in distinctive ways, for example, to say nothing of the potential contribution of Orthodox Christianity.

Far from a glitzy import, then, Christian Democracy is made of solid, familiar stuff—the stuff that Christians have long wrestled with in various places and at different times. Essentially, it calls for an authentic obedience to the living God. All over the world, Christians face the same issues in relation to public responsibility. We are to love God and love our neighbor as ourselves. Rather than treat the American or European solutions as disconnected, Christians everywhere ought to be learning to share their common *Christian* heritage in these several struggles. The churches we belong to are one with the universal church. We ought to pursue solidarity with one another as members of the body of Christ. It is vital that the parts serve the whole, of course, but no less important for the parts to be sustained by the whole. That is the spirit in which we commend the principles of Christian Democracy to American Christians.

Strategic Considerations

As we draw our arguments to a close, we are well aware of the strategic difficulties presented by our prescriptions. Christian Democracy in the United States is at best underdeveloped, its vocabulary unfamiliar to American ears. The rich deposits of Catholic thought lie largely hidden from a general audience, and the more sympathetic Protestant efforts are confined to a small one.[8] But we have to take this opportunity to remind our readers of the strategy we have advocated throughout this book. Doing politics Christianly, we argue, begins necessarily in churches. One sort of church familiar to North American Christians produces a piecemeal politics of passionate, spasmodic, amateurish reforms tinged with a strong distrust of the political arena as a place for Christian activity. Another kind—one we believe to be more faithful to the New Testament conception of the church as the body of Christ—produces a no less passionate but more engaged politics, whose concern for justice embraces ongoing administration as much as periodic reform, and whose view of the political arena is reflected in its insistence that the sovereign God calls us to his service in all walks of life.

So we end where we began, in churches. But what then? There are, it has been argued, three major conditions under which European Christian Democracy established itself: First, there was conflict, an attack or series of attacks on the church, which served to unite Christians in resistance; second, there arose a well-developed theory or ideology to draw together Christian insights and principles, to work through objections and problems, and to translate principles to policy; and third, a well-educated and receptive audience gave its support to the movement.[9]

The first of these conditions is the subject of some debate in the United States. Arguably, however, the rise of the Christian right in the 1980s was indicative of the displacement of Christian values in American society, itself a condition, if not an actual manifestation, of hostility. Richard John Neuhaus, writing in *First Things,* regularly catalogs individual examples of hostile acts directed toward Christians by public authorities or tolerated by those authorities. The struggles being fought at the local level over issues such as sex education in schools, the distribution of condoms, and so forth, probably provide the best litmus test of popular and official attitudes.

If our analysis is accurate, the second condition—formation of a well-developed ideology—has not been met, especially by evangelicals, whose traditions, position in society, and view of Scripture have underplayed development of a Christian ideology. American Christians for the most part have not anticipated an engaged Christian presence in the public sphere. Developing such an ideology lies well beyond the scope of this book, so we have attempted instead to show how Christians in churches might begin the task. The Christian Democratic tradition may then open up as a rich mine of resources to be consulted for insight, encouragement, education, and direction. The great importance of this tradition for a nation like the United States is that it preserves a way of thinking about state and society unfamiliar to most Americans while keeping for them a means of establishing a truly substantial political independence passing well beyond a rejection of current liberal and neoconservative formulas. On examination, Christian Democracy possesses even higher standards of freedom than those embodied in the American Constitution, as it addresses those central questions about people and society and political power that Americans faced in the eighteenth century. Christian Democracy resolves those questions in ways that Americans, who care deeply about freedom, ought to examine with care.

The third condition, a well-educated and receptive audience, is the one we have paid most attention to in this book. We have written especially for local congregations, imagining groups of Christians sitting down to tackle questions of public responsibility and needing a guide. It is our hope that this book will serve as the kind of guide that can give hope to those already convinced that something is wrong with the orientation of many churches to these questions. We hope you will tell us what has helped and what needs to be rewritten.

In conclusion, readers should be aware that we have steered clear of a full-length treatment of Christian Democracy. Indeed, we avoided any discussion of it at all until the end of the book. Why? We wished to avoid imposing a perspective from above, whole and undigested as it were, in contradiction of the book's method and our convictions about just how much can be homegrown by groups of Christians tackling these matters from a biblical point of view. And as we have shown, the issues that produced Christian Democracy are shared widely by the body of Christ—a homegrown, American response to them is quite conceivable. Finally, to try to impose Christian Democracy on others would be contrary to its own practices, which, being personalist, seek to empower, protect, and liberate people in the multiple relationships in which they live their lives. Once groups of Christians have started to tackle these questions for themselves, however, a study of Christian Democracy promises to be a very fruitful next step to take.

The authors *are* convinced Christian Democrats! So it is appropriate that we should nail our colors to the mast in the final chapter. While we do not reject other approaches to public responsibility—radical or realist—we are convinced that the view of people, community, society, church and state, and above all of the sovereign, redeeming love of God presented in these pages, is a biblical one. It is a view that happens also to win strong affirmation among those who have called themselves Christian Democrats. So we conclude, not so much by pointing our readers in a Christian Democratic direction as by pointing out to them that the direction taken in these pages may fairly be described as Christian Democratic. Perhaps readers may then, as we have, draw encouragement from the resulting reconnections to the Christian struggle to do justice, to love mercy, and to walk humbly with God (see Mic. 6:8).

STUDY QUESTIONS

1. According to the authors, what are the troublesome features of contemporary liberal democracy in the United States? What do you think?
2. Discuss the authors' view that some kind of character training is especially important for citizens in a democracy like the United States.
3. Discuss the idea that Christian communities, not simply Christian believers having Christian values, are indispensable to democracy.
4. How can Christians contribute to public debate without "imposing" their values on a pluralistic society? (You may wish to discuss how pluralistic American society really is.)
5. The authors argue that Christian Democracy challenges and transforms the categories of liberal democracy in a manner that is biblically faithful. Do you agree? How important is such a challenge and transformation?
6. What steps should your church or study group take next?

Notes

Chapter 1: Sojourners and Citizens

1. Evangelical Christians were at work in all the great social movements of the last century, and it is a thousand pities that this history is not better known among evangelicals. Helpful works on the subject include George M. Marsden, *Fundamentalism and American Culture: The Shaping of Twentieth Century Evangelicalism, 1870–1925* (New York: Oxford University Press, 1980); David Bebbington, *Evangelicalism in Modern Britain* (New York: Unwin Hyman, 1989).

Chapter 2: Taking Our Bearings from the Kingdom

1. Marty employs these metaphors to describe the emergence of fundamentalism in the early years of the twentieth century. It always comes as something of a shock to learn that this allegedly conservative theology was in fact a creative innovation no more than eighty years ago. Martin E. Marty, *Modern American Religion, Vol. 1, The Irony of It All, 1893–1919* (Chicago: University of Chicago Press, 1986). See also Robert Bellah, et al., *Habits of the Heart: Individualism and Commitment in American Life* (New York: Harper, 1985), and James Hunter, *Evangelicalism: The Coming Generation* (Chicago: University of Chicago Press, 1987).

2. Robert Farrar Capon, *The Parables of the Kingdom* (Grand Rapids: Eerdmans, 1985), 27.

3. Ibid., 73.

4. Ibid., 81.

Chapter 3: Setting Sail in the Church

1. Robert Webber, *The Church in the World* (Grand Rapids: Zondervan, 1986), 284.

2. Ibid.

3. At the time of writing, an "Episcopal synod" has come into existence in the United States, grouping together congregations who reject the theological positions of their own geographical dioceses or of the national church. Significantly, the organizational basis of the new synod is not geography, but belief.

4. Richard Baer has written with insight on the consequences of the public equation of "religious" with "sectarian." See Richard A. Baer, Jr., "The Supreme Court's Discriminatory Use of the Term 'Sectarian,'" *The Journal of Law and Politics* (Spring 1990), 449–68.

Chapter 4: Beyond Piecemeal Politics

1. Christopher Townsend and Michael Schluter, *Why Keep Sunday Special?* (Cambridge: Jubilee Publications, 1985), 83.

2. Our own debts are greatest to Reformed thinkers, among them Rockne McCarthy, James Skillen, and Robert Webber, and to the tradition of Dutch neo-Calvinism in which they stand.

Chapter 5: Overcoming the Language Barrier

1. For a full account of Jesse Jackson's public theology, see Roger D. Hatch, "Jesse Jackson in Two Worlds," in Charles Dunn, ed., *Religion in American Politics* (Washington, D.C.: Congressional Quarterly Press, 1989).

2. Christopher J. Wright, *An Eye for an Eye: The Place of Old Testament Ethics Today* (Downers Grove, Ill.: InterVarsity Press, 1983), 198.

3. J. N. Figgis, "Political Thought from Gerson to Grotius, 1414–1625" (quoted in James W. Skillen and Rockne M. McCarthy, ed., *Political Order and the Plural Structure of Society* (Atlanta: Scholars Press, 1991), 106.

4. The six principles are discussed in full in David Alton, *Faith in Britain* (London: Hodder, 1991), and Alan Storkey, *Towards Christian Democracy* (London: CSP, 1990). Both may be obtained from the Movement for Christian Democracy, c/o David Alton, MP, House of Commons, London SW1A OAA, England.

5. Storkey, *Towards Christian Democracy*, 41.

Chapter 6: Christian Principles for Politics

1. See Nathan Hatch, "The Democratization of Christianity, and the Character of American Politics," in Mark Noll, ed., *Religion and American Politics: From the Colonial Period to the 1980s* (New York: Oxford University Press, 1990).

2. The Ninth and Tenth Amendments to the Constitution seem to provide excellent limits to federal power, but the Supreme Court has been very

reluctant to use them to protect the integrity of states when conflicts have arisen. Important cases in the recent past are *National League of Cities v. Usery* 426 U.S. 833 (1976) and *Garcia v. San Antonio Metropolitan Transit Authority* 469 U.S. 528 (1985).

3. Stephen E. Fowl and L. Gregory Jones, *Reading in Communion: Scripture and Ethics in Christian Life* (Grand Rapids: Eerdmans, 1991).

4. Why don't we just call American society a communitarian society and advocate a communitarian democracy, as Amitai Etzioni and others in the "communitarian movement" have done recently? Isn't a recovery of community precisely the antidote that a narcissistic society needs? We must distinguish pluralist democracy from communitarian democracy, however. Communitarian democracy assumes that society (made up as it is of lots of communities, organizations, persons, families, regions, religions, and so forth) may be designated a community and have community norms developed for it. We think this is facile. Pluralist democracy would resist calling a loose grouping of communities a community. Just policy can be made only if the integrity of each smaller unit is respected. See Etzioni, *The Spirit of Community: Rights, Responsibilities, and the Communitarian Agenda* (New York: Crown, 1993).

5. The foundations of Roman Catholic social thought lie in the teachings of Thomas Aquinas, who gave it its distinctive shape and familiar basic principles.

6. Michael Fogarty, "The Churches and Public Policy," *Political Quarterly* 63, no. 3 (1992): 301–6.

7. What preserved Locke's vision of society from anarchy may well have been his belief in humanity's reasonableness; yet if humans are predisposed to cooperate, perhaps there was no need to go to all the trouble of drafting an elaborate social contract to persuade them to do so.

8. The organization closest to the MCD in the United States is the older Association for Public Justice, whose intellectual and theological roots lie in Dutch neo-Calvinism, notably the work of Abraham Kuyper and Herman Dooyeweerd, and whose public philosophy approaches Christian Democracy from this direction. The Center for Public Justice is directed by James Skillen. Center for Public Justice, P.O. Box 48368, Washington, D.C. 20002.

9. Michael Fogarty, *Christian Democracy in Western Europe, 1820–1953* (London: Routledge, 1957).